Sean Ingram International

Africa - Asia - Europe - The Americas

This book is a work of fiction. Names, characters, places, and incidents are either products of the author's imagination or are used fictitiously.

Any resemblance to actual events or locales or persons, living or dead, is entirely coincidental.

Published by:
Sean Ingram, Inc.
P.O. Box 28131
Raleigh, NC 27611

Library of Congress
ISBN: 0-9749049-3-7

Printed in the United States of America

The basis of the story can be read 'Within' the lines that have been written, but yet the meaning of the story can only be read 'Between' the lines that have been written. So therefore, in order to understand the true meaning of the story, you must close your eyes and open your mind.

-Sean Ingram

-Author's Note-

This book has intentionally been written for the intellectual thinker. Many of the works within this collection have been written in riddles that you may mentally put the questionable puzzle together yourself. I challenge you to think as you read, and become the author of your own conclusions of each piece of literature.

Please be aware that each word has been carefully placed, so what may seem an incorrection, or a word out of context, may actually be a word of diversion, purposely used to draw more thought within a moment of confusion.

So I challenge you to challege yourself, as well as others, that you may decipher the codes of my eccentric thoughts.

Quotes & Haikus

If you Hate Me, then I Love You,
for you're my Motivation
But if you Love Me, then I Thank You,
for you're my Inspiration

~~~~~~

Her smile sung to me
Her voice as the melody
For her song was Love

~~~~~~

One should be proud to be Black,
for Black is the essence of all that has been,
and all that is to come

~~~~~~

My heart is broken
And my tears no longer fall
But yet I still smile

~~~~~~

Heaven is her name
Angelic is her Essence
For she's my Black Queen

~~~~~~

Nature is Crying
For her tears fall from her eyes
As Rain From Heaven
~~~~~~

How can one wrap their arms around,
and truly embrace their future
If their hands are preoccupied by
holding on to the problems of their past?

~~~~~~~~~~~~~~~~~~~~~~~~~~~~~~~~~~~~~

Loves hurts, just as love heals,
but only a fool loves to be hurt,
and declines healing

~~~~~~~~~~~~~~~~~~~~~~~~~~~~~~~~~~~~~

Black as the Mid-night
Radiant as the Noon Sun
For She's AFRICA

~~~~~~~~~~~~~~~~~~~~~~~~~~~~~~~~~~~~~

The young are crying
But no one other than God
Seems to hear their Plea

~~~~~~~~~~~~~~~~~~~~~~~~~~~~~~~~~~~~~

Beautiful she is
Truly a sight to behold
For She Is Black Gold

~~~~~~~~~~~~~~~~~~~~~~~~~~~~~~~~~~~~~

Lies only become harmful when used
or applied in a misguided or negative manner,
Otherwise, lies are only an expression
of one's creativity and imagination
~~~~~~~~~~~~~~~~~~~~~~~~~~~~~~~~~~~~~

Time could either be Beneficial or Detrimental,
Therefore, you must take advantage of time,
or else, time will surely take advantage of you

~~~~~~

Life Abandoned me
Death became Reality
Henceforth I am FREE

~~~~~~

Yesterday is gone
Tomorrow may never come
So I'll Seize Today

~~~~~~

Life raced right past me
As summer days became cold
For Hell has Frozen

~~~~~~

Dreams are only fantasies,
that in time become Reality

And because of this,

I have become the Writer of my dreams,
only because you have chosen to be my reader

So I Sincerely Thank You!

~~~~~~

My Soul is my Throne
For Gods Kingdome is my Home
Thus I am a King

~~~~~~

He is Me Reborn
Son of the Son of the Sun
For He too is Light

Dream a Dream
That will never be forgotten

Visualize a Vision
That will forever be seen

Live a Life
That you may always be remembered

Die a Death
That you may eternally live serene

So continue to be...

I Dedicate this book to writers of every genre whom have came before me, bleeding their creative ideas and emotional passions via the ink of their pen, for you have opened the door for me, that I may leave the door open for the future generations of writers whom are to come.

-Sean Ingram

The Love I Lost...

I will forever miss you,
for you were truly one of a kind

For it was only you who gave me the keys
to open the doors for my ideas,
allowing me to free the sporadic thoughts
that I held captured in my mind

I remember when I first told you that I was a writer,
and you said that it must have been destiny,
because writing was also your first love

We then became so close,
that you began finishing my sentences
with the exact same words
that I had just been thinking of

I couldn't help releasing my passion to you,
as I stroked you gently
with every emotion that my heart revealed

confiding in you my deepest secrets,
even the numerous untold secrets,
that I have always kept concealed

And forever will I thank you for interceding,
for it was you who bridged the gap
between my many thoughts and the empty sheets

But unfortunately as time has once again proven,
all good things must one day become obsolete

Even you,
My Dearly Departed Typewriter...

Contents

-Chapter Six-
(When Hell Appears As Heaven)

-Chapter Seven-
(When Death Becomes Life)

Booking Information
&
Other Books Available by Sean Ingram

Please visit us at www.SeanIngram.info and post your thoughts of this book at our Critics Corner, also become a member of our online book club.

"When Dreams Become Reality"

The Artistically Eccentric...

The bristles of her brush erratically stroked the canvas, transferring from mind to manifestation the conceptions of her sporadic thoughts.

Tears of confusion cried from within her paintbrush onto the coarse cloth of her life, as she unconsciously commenced to commingling the hues of love, hate, joy, sorrow, courage, and fear into a collage of frantic harmony.

The subliminal implications of her intricate painting overshadowed the beauty of her astonishing masterpiece, enticing a jury of world renowned artistic scholars to expertise the complexity of her anomalous artistry.

"Eccentrically Astounding" the artistic intellectuals proclaimed, as they exhaustively attempted to dissect the perplexity within the simplicity of a schizophrenic mind.

<u>Empathically Engaged...</u>

The Essence of her somatically imprisoned his soul, enslaving his very being to her naturally inherited sensual femininity.

Obsessively intrigued by her effeminate nature, he perceptually became as one with her, envisioning mental mirages through the perspective of her eyes.

Emulating her pains with his song, he mimicked her lifes melody in the falsetto of his altoic voice.

" I am she, for she is a part of me" he proclaimed, empathically defending their aberrant bond as he stands before the smoky mirror of her reflection.

<u>A Long Walk To Nowhere...</u>

After twelve long years of anxiously waiting, death has finally come knocking on my door.
Though he was hours away, I could still hear his
footsteps even though it seemed as if he was walking
on floors made of the softest cotton. As the time
would continue to remissly elapse, anxiety would
begin to conquer my mind, body, and soul. His
footsteps appeared to perfectly coincide with the
rhythmic beats of my dismal heart. My mind fell into
a state of dreaded shock, and though I remained
conscious, it seemed as if my paralyzed body could
do nothing as I laid awake in a coma.

Step-by-step, inch-by-inch, and second-by-
second, death continuously made his way to me,
that he may soon vanquish my contrite soul. Silence
smothered my cell as my thoughts of hope became
ineffectual. It appeared the closer he would get to

me, the more I was able to hear, not only his footsteps, but now I was beginning to catch sound of his placid breathing sequence, and from that alone, I could tell that he was in no rush at all to introduce me to the perpetuity of darkness.

The shadows of memory began to cloud my mind as I continued to anxiously wait for death to knock at my door. My life passed before me as my thoughts drifted aimlessly to the days of my childhood. I unconsciously began to reminisce on the days I use to sit on the porch with my grandfather enjoying the cool breeze on a hot summer day and the sweet smell of freshly cut grass. I would begin to hear his voice saying to me that life was as a vapor, meaning that, life, just as a vapor, would only exist for a moment, and then would be gone forever in just an blink of an eye. I forgot whom he quoted that from, but never the less, I found it to be so true in the years to come.

As my thoughts continued to randomly travel until

briefly halting at a day within my adolescent life. Vague images began to become somewhat intelligible as the clouded visions in which encompassed my troubled mind began to be understood in great clarity. I remembered being at the young age of eleven years old, and though many years has since elapsed, it is as if it was only yesterday. I can still hear the gentle voice of my grandmother saying to me that life would be nothing more than a test administered by God until our final day of judgment, where as our reward would be eternal heaven or our reprimand would be eternal hell. I began to meditate on the words that she so sincerely spoke to me, and it was then that I realized that my life had indeed been nothing more than a test, and because of the decisions that I had made in the past, whether it be good or bad, I have now come to confront the unyielding moment of Gods judgment.

It seemed as though someone was standing afar softly whispering my name. The voice was polite and comforting, but yet and still, so profound that it quivered my uneasy soul. I then heard pounding sounds as if they were massive waves crashing against the boulders of a mountain, in which I misconceived with the throbbing of my heart. My eyes hastily opened, as my comatose state of being quickly faded away. "Jackson it's time", the voice outside of the door stated to me, which also said without saying, that death has finally come. The sound of jingling keys startled me, because it was then that I realized that the locks on the door would not be enough to cause death to cease.

I sat up on my bunk as the door opened. My eyes gazed towards the door that they may greet death as soon as he entered my single man cell. My eyes then suddenly blinked, and when they reopened, there in front of me stood not the face of death, but that of his accomplice. "It's time Jackson, are you ready?", He asked me as he pulled a pair of handcuffs from his utility belt. His words pierced my soul and left me almost lifeless as if I was a vampire and a wooden stake had just been driven into the center of my heart. My head dropped down, only to look back up and see that twelve years of dreams has now become reality.

Every night for the past twelve years I have anxiously awaited for death to come knocking on my door, and now the time has finally come. "Death awaits", the officer eyes said to me without him ever saying a single word. Now cuffed and fettered, we began the long walk to what I considered as nowhere. As we journeyed, my mind once again began to aimlessly travel back to the days of my yesteryears. My life passed before my eyes in just a matter of minutes, only to be interrupted by the opening of a door which led to my final destination. Once through the door, we were greeted by the chaplain, who was accompanied by the warden and some others whom I had never seen before. A shocking chill ran down the spine of my back as if the temperature had dropped increasingly from that of my cell.

"Mr. Jackson?" the chaplain asked as I stood motionless before him with only one thing on my mind. "Yes", I replied as I went on to ask him if he thought God would forgive me for what I had done. He just looked at me speechless for a moment until he finally commented on my question. "Well Mr. Jackson, I don't think there's too much that you can do that God won't forgive you for If you sincerely repent to him from the bottom of your heart", the chaplain explained to me as the officers sat me down in the chair in which I would never walk away from. By the look on the chaplain's face, I could tell that he was expecting me to request one final phone call or something of that sort, but in all actuality, I had no one to call. Unconsciously, a smile came across my face as I wondered why was it that they always asked you would you want a final meal, as if it really mattered.

My teary eyes gazed the room only to find myself within the mirror on the wall before me. Though I could not see them, I could hear their silent sighs as they anxiously awaited for death to enter the room, just as I did. The chaplain patiently waited in the corner of the room beside the red phone which hung on the wall as if he was waiting on God to call to prevent death from retrieving me. Within the mirror before me, I could see the chaplain raise his right hand while holding up his pointer finger as if he was indicating to those that mattered, he would only wait one more minute for that red phone to ring. Second by second, the minute quickly faded away. The chaplain nodded his head, silently saying without mumbling a word, that it was now time.

As I was approached by the nurse whom was accompanied by two more officers, my eyes closed only to see death standing before me. "I'm going to give you three shots Mr. Jackson", the tenderly pleasant voice of the young nurse said to me, as she began preparing my arm to receive my first of the last touches of a woman.

My body quivered as the pinch of the first shot startled me. Though my eyes were clenched closed, tears found a way to seep through and form a gradual stream from the corners of my eyes to the bottom of my chin. My rapid heart beat began to stagnate, as my asthmatic breathing sequence slowly tapered. Once again, shadows of memories began to cloud my mind as if I was day dreaming. Despite the situation at hand, I began to feel extremely re-laxed, feeling as if I had just taken a bubble bath in a tub full of chamomile tea. What once felt as anxiety attacks, was now beginning to seem as a peaceful truce between my mind, body, and soul.

Being that I was so at ease, I barely even felt the pinch of the second shot. I tried to open my eyes, but my eyelids were so heavy that I couldn't find the strength to unveil the darkness. A hush fell over me as my consciousness slowly drifted away. It seemed as if it was a dream, but even if it was, I knew it was one that I would never awake from. "Mr. Jackson, It's time", a mans voice softly said to me. Though his

face was vague in visibility, his presence alone allowed me to know that he was indeed the very one
that I have been anxiously awaiting for the past
twelve years of my incarcerated life.

Death had finally come and introduced himself
to me. Though I had dreamed of this moment for
many years, never once did I imagine that it would be
so serene. It seemed as if I stood before the ocean
listening to the sounds of the waves within the sea-
shell of my mind. It was just him and me, face to face
at last. "Follow me", death instructed as he turned
and walked ahead of me through the haze of clouds
which surrounded us. I followed as he requested,
while wondering where exactly it was that we were
going. He must have read my mind, for he promptly
answered my unasked question by telling me that we
were going before the council that would ultimately
determine my fate.

It was reminiscent like it was dejavu, being that here I was once again standing before a judges bench. The last time, I was sentenced to death, so I now pondered the unlikely possibility of me being sentenced to life this go around.

Out of the corner of my eye, I could see the familiar face of death whom was the bailiff. As I looked behind me, I noticed that Jesus would be my attorney, while on the other side of the court room, the district attorney would be none other that Satan himself.

"All rise for the Honorable God Almighty", the bailiff announced as God walked through the pearly gates and took his throne.

I stood paralyzed as the voices of Jesus and Satan negotiated my lively deeds. The closing arguments had been presented, and now God was prepared to disclose his decision. My final destination had been determined, and all I could do was once again anxiously wait on the verdict to be announced, wondering would it be eternal life or death.

The Truth Unveiled...

What I thought to be Trials and Tribulations,
was actually the misunderstanding of God's lessons

And that which I thought was Heart Ache and Pains,
was only the preparations for God's blessings

For my Loneliness,
served as quality time with my heavenly father

And that of Misery,
proved to be mental training,
for when times would become much harder

Just as Neglection,
was God's way of molding me to be a man

And that I considered as Abandonment,
was indeed God's teachings,
that I may one day grow to comprehend,
what It is that I have now learned to understand

Which is the story of my life is not my own,
For God is the Author

<u>Outside, Looking in...</u>

My soul transcended from my being, allowing me to observe the essence of myself from an celestial horizon.

Studiously I searched for myself within the mist of millions, scanning the earth over within a blink of an eye.

"Where am I?" I confusedly questioned my guardian angel, as I continued to look the world over.

"Right there" he replied, directing my focus upon a man that had no resemblance of that of myself.

"That can't be me" I thought to myself, closely analyzing the man that was brought to my undivided attention.

"Yes, that's you" he softly said, answering my unspoken thoughts. "But your view is different now, for you are now viewing yourself from outside-in, instead of Inside-out. Being that you have never seen yourself in this way, you don't recognize yourself, for you're not seeing yourself as you always have in life, but rather the way in which others have always viewed you." He continued to explain to me in a most intriguing manner.

I stood silently dumb-founded as my overwhelmed mind raced to catch grasp of the loose pieces from his puzzling information. My gazing eyes perused every inch of the man whom was said to be me, and from every dissecting aspect, I still could not see what was being seen through the eyes of others.

"In order for you to see what they see, you must close your eyes and open your mind." He said, "For then and only then will you truly be able to see the true you" He continued to tell me as he placed his hand over my eyes, darkening my vision while enlightening my thoughts.

"This is who you are" He told me as I envisioned a prestigiously powerful and wealthy man. "But this is the man whom you see daily within the mirror" He said, taking his hands from before my eyes, allowing me to once again see that Insignificant man that I have always been accustomed to.

"So is it true that I'm that great man?" I asked, as my voice screamed with skepticism in such a moderate mono toned manner.

"Indeed you are a mighty man of valor" He assured me, "But you have been educationally miseducated to believe otherwise by those to whom you pose a threat."

"But why do I oppose a threat to anyone?" I curiously inquired, yearning for the wisdom that fell from his lips with each word he spoke.

"Because they know your greatness, as well as your potential. They also know, that if you knew the true you, then no longer could you be mentally contained" He continued to enlighten me on thoughts I have never fathomed.

"You are the reflection of God, for you are as a lighthouse unto the lost . Your voice is heavy as a mighty brass horn, and your mind is as illustrious as

the Sun. Your intricate nature is that of a black panther, for you also are silently elegant, intriguingly
attractive, while simultaneously being exceptionally
deadly. Socially, you're an aristocrat." He revealed
to me, continuing to shed light on the darkness
which I had always befriended.

"Do you recognize him now?" He questioned, directing my attention to the man within the reflection
of his hand.

"Yes" I answered, "He's the man whom they never
wanted me to know, for he is the man which God has
destined me to be," I proclaimed with a smile.

"This is true my son, and the truth can never be
denied" He assured me with an reciprocating smile
upon his face as he embraced me within arms of
undoubted sincerity.

"So go now and be the man in which you have
always been" My angel encouraged me as our souls
departed, mine descending back into the earthly
realm, and his transcending back into the heavens
from which he had come.

On Earth, as it is in Hell...

Overwhelming agony burns deep within my despondent soul, encompassing my impious essence with unbearable torment.

Infuriating frustrations ignites my irritable emotions, compelling me to become enslaved unto my irrational thoughts.

Teary lakes of lava exudes though the crevices of the broken dams within my eyes, perniciously flooding the depths of my emotional abyss.

Panic devoured my last taste of hope, digesting my optimism into the corrosive acids of hells belly.

Rage regurgitated obscene profanity, wrathfully damning the very creator of creation, thus condemning my scrutinized soul to the eternal utopian after life of sinful bliss.

Contempt engulfs my chaotic consciousness, coercing me to contemplate existence or extinction, for surely after death, there can be no worse experience of hell, than that of here on earth.

When Death Comes...

When Death Comes...

I'll embrace him with open arms,
and thank him for finally coming

I'll look him directly in his eyes,
and boldly tell him that I'm tired of running

I'll stand face to face with him,
to let him know that I'm proud to die as a man

I'll reach out to him as a martyr,
awaiting the moment he accepts my extended hand

For wise men seeks wise council,
so when he speaks of the after life,
I'll anxiously listen

For his prophecy proclaims to me,
that death is only my poetic beginning

<u>The Hands of Time...</u>

Tomorrow seems as if it will never come,
and yesterday seems so far away

So now I feel as if I am trapped in time,
wandering aimlessly just trying to find my way

Not knowing where it is that I am going,
while trying to remember,
from where it is that I have come

Seeing so many faces along the way,
but only vaguely recognizing some

I am hearing voices in my head,
while seeing mirages through my eyes

The earth is falling beneath my feet,
just as above my head is the falling skies

Life and Death seems to be as one,
as the Moon has eclipsed the Sun

It is then that I close my eyes,
only to see that all is not done

So I must Live On

<u>Cry No More...</u>

When my soul departs from the soil of my being,
and the air that was manifested into the breathe of
life detours away from my lungs and returns to God.

Please Don't Shed Any Tears

For when I was an adolescent, and I cried out to
you for help, you didn't cry with me, nor did you
care to comfort me, so therefor, when the North
Star falls from the sky.

Please Don't Shed Any Tears

For when the strife of my teenaged life imbued
my being with overwhelming anguish, you never attempted to console me, for you only observed me
from a distance with pointed fingers, so therefore,
when the Earth crumbles beneath your feet.

Please Don't Shed Any Tears

For when I needed you as an adult, you forsook me, leaving me alone with no one but the child that cried within me, so therefore, when the Sun no longer shines in the morning.

Please Don't Shed any Tears

So please, when my soul departs from the soil of my being, and the air that was manifested into the breathe of life detours away from my lungs and returns to God.

Please Don't Shed Any Tears

For you didn't cry for me while I was living,
So why cry for me when I'm Dead

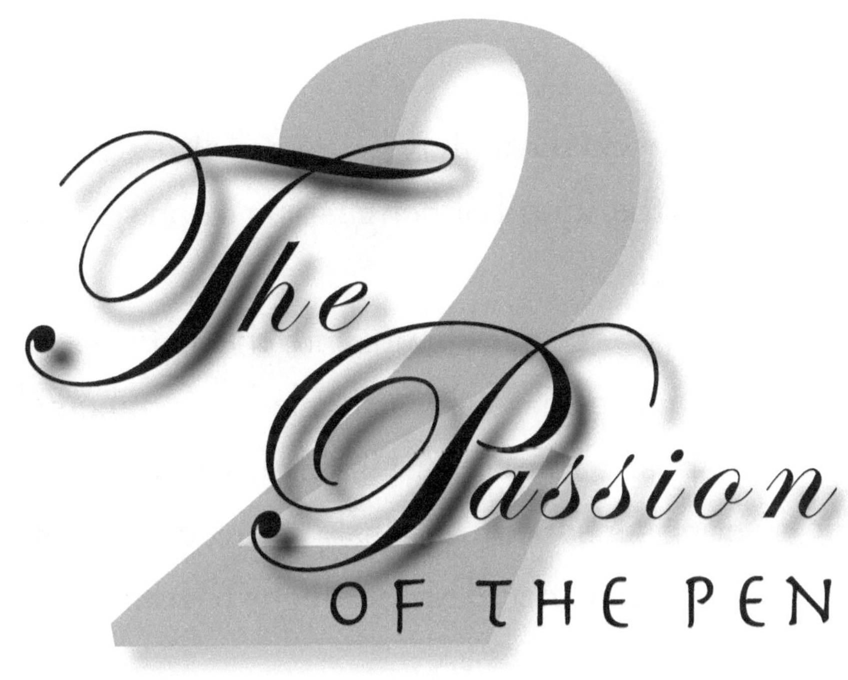

"When The Ink Imitates Your Imagination"

Her First Time...

Tears escaped through the crevices of her squinting eyes, as the sound of her gasping moans gradually increased.

Her fingertips began clawing into the mattress in which she laid upon, as she struggled to free herself from the spastic pain of him inside of her.

Quivering sensations aimlessly traveled through her body, causing her elevated thighs to tremble sporadically.

Anxiety seized the essence of her being, as her internal senses indicated that he was soon to come.

A silent sigh of relief escaped through her lips, as the sound of his voice bestowed upon her a peace of mind.

"It's a healthy baby boy", the doctor cheerfully announced, as he held her very first new born child in his hands.

For The Love of You...

If loving you as I do was against the will of God,
then surely, Hell would be my final destination

For without you, life would be meaningless,
therefore, I will accept death without hesitation

Thus, I will yearn for you eternally,
longing to hold serenity,
within the chastisement of my demise

I'll have nightmares of...
tasting the sweetness of your lips,
and being blinded for glimpsing into heaven,
within the beauty of your angelic eyes

I'll go deaf listening for the sound of your voice,
and dumb for constantly calling out your name

For this would be my suffering for loving you,
thereby causing Hell and Earth to be as the same

For what greater curse,
could God bestow upon me in life,
Than That Of Being Without You

<u>Passenger 21...</u>

"All Aboard!", the conductor shouted as I kissed my mother goodbye, grabbed held of my bags, and hurried to board the train which had patiently awaited.

"You have a pleasant trip sir", the nice man said to me in the most hospitable way after checking my ticket and the tags on my luggage.

"Thank you sir", I generously replied to him, while making my way onto the train of life.

Once aboard, I scurried down the aisle attempting to avoid baggage collisions with my fellow passengers, while searching to find the seat which has been designated for passenger twenty-seven. As I bobbed and weaved my way through the crowded aisle-way, I accidently bumped into a female passenger that struggled to place her belongings into the overhead storage compartment.

"Excuse me, let me help you", I apologized to the woman while lifting her bags from out of her hands, and placing them into the baggage compartment.

"Thank you", her soft voice whispered in my ear as I began to search for my seat again.

Unloaded and situated, I flopped into my seat and mentally settled in. Just as I became somewhat comfortable, a distorted bass-filled voice blared through the speakers of the intercom.

"Your next stop will....", I heard the voice say before being distracted by the waving hand of my mother whom was still standing on the dock of the train station.

While returning my mothers wave, the brakes released its' steam, the engine revved, and the train slowly began to pull off into the cloudy haze of spiritual existence.

Anxiety overwhelmed my being as the train began to travel its journey through life. My subconscious thoughts attempted to envision the inevitable fate of my final destination as I gazed out the window into the premonitions of tomorrow and the years to come, only to find myself starring back at myself within the reflection of the window.

Hypnotized by my somnolent thoughts and the harmonic hum of the trains engine, my wide eyes grew heavy, overbearing my will to stay awoke.

"Pardon me sir", the little boy sitting next to me said, expressing his regrets for accidently awakening me as he removed his bags from the storage compartment and peacefully exited the train without leaving a trace of his presence.

"The seventh station", I mumbled to myself in bewilderment as I looked out my window and read the stations welcoming billboard.

Silently I sat, Pondering the explanation of why it is that the little boy who seemed so innocent, had reached his destination in life so soon.

While perusing the aisle to trace the unseen tracks of the little boy within my memories, I noticed a strikingly beautiful woman glancing back at me from the twenty-first passenger seat.

We greeted each other with pleasant smiles, as our gazing eyes introduced us without ever uttering a single word.

"Nice to meet you", we both silently spoke to the other, via the blushing smiles that illuminated our ebony faces.

Telepathically, we danced to the songs of love in perfect harmony, gracefully complementing each other step by step.

Our hearts fluttered with infatuation, as our gazing eyes successfully penetrated the soul of the other.

"I declare you as soulmates", the voice of God spoke upon us through the speaker, spiritually uniting us as unconditional companions.

"Oh what a pleasant journey this should be", I thought to myself, never imagining the emotional derailment that was soon to come.

Confusion seized my mind and heart as the gesture of her hand altered from hello to goodbye. My rapid thoughts curiously pondered the significance of her implications, before being answered by the sight of her hand slowly falling from the sky, to gently gripping the straps of her handbag.

It seemed as if I could feel the pulsation of my heart gradually decrease as I intensely observed her retrieve her belongings from where they once resided.

"Excuse me miss!", I called out to her to no avail as she gracefully made her way towards the exit with luggage in hand.

"But why?", I asked myself, invoking an answer from God as I peeked out my window and viewed the billboard which read "The 14th Station"

Once again I silently sat perusing the aisle attempting to trace the unseen tracks of the angel whom will forever be remembered as passenger 21.

-Authors Note-

This short story is an elaboration of the poem " Alone on the Am Trak" from the book "Tears of a Empty Pen".

This narrative of invented prose is dedicated to my dearly departed friend, Lakeisha Sneed, whom I only had the chance to know briefly before her passing from the disease of leukemia at the age of 14. Also in the memory of Patricia "PAT" Suggs.

<u>Naturally So...</u>

The clouds poured out its' love upon me
and washed away my pain,
While iridescent colors striped the sky,
during the presence of the rain

A gentle breeze consoled my soul
as I gazed into the rising sun,
While the tears of mama nature embraced me,
as if I was her only son

Whispering winds sung melodies
within my invoking ears,
As the rays of the rising sun,
dried my falling tears

My heart cried out unto the mother,
as the skies began to blush
While the voice of the peaceful ocean,
pleaded with my crying heart to hush

My heart smiled as mama nature
nurtured my despondent soul,
For within the skies her heavenly eyes,
I could see the manifestation of my life unfold

<u>Intimately Immanent...</u>

Conceptual perceptions,
allowed my mind to draw a silhouette,
of your slim waist and protruding hips

A kiss brought your figmentation to life,
as your kiss manifested mental mirages,
of honey dew dripping from your lips

A glimpse into your beautiful eyes,
revealed to me with such clarity,
an eternal glimpse of heavens perfection

Your gentle touch fused my senses,
sending me into the shock,
of an mental erection

The sound of your voice seemed as humming birds,
while whispering sweet melodies,
accompanied by the soft percussion,
of the drums within my ears

Intercourse had intercoursed our souls,
thus declaring us as soulmates,
through the course of our infinite years

But even if not,
Oh What A Blissful Dream...

<u>Natural Telepathy...</u>

Just the other day, the winds whispered within my ears, as the clouds sprinkled upon me your dis-tressed tears to inform me that you were not at all doing so well.

As I meditated on the pulsations of your heart, I could faintly hear how hard the ills of life had been beating upon your despondent soul.

Still attentively listening to your inner being, I could hear your heart convulsively gasping, while desperately struggling to grasp for only a moments breath of fresh air.

Therefore I whispered back within the winds, requesting the favor that your lungs be filled with divine inspiration.

Then I called upon the clouds, requesting that

they move from before the sun which radiantly
awaited behind them, that the sun may shine upon
you the love in which your longing heart desires.

Lastly I called upon the eagles, requesting that
they keep a keen eye out for the first sight of any
trouble that may attempt to come your way.

Henceforth, just yesterday, the winds whispered
once again within my ears to notify me that your
frown has now turned into a beautiful smile.

The clouds showered me with your tears of joy, as
vibrant colors illuminated the sky, reflecting peacefully within the rays of the sun.

As I stood mesmerized by the serenity within
the beauty of nature, all I could was ponder such a
simple thought, for oh what a beautiful sight it is to
see you happy my beloved.

<u>Dawn...</u>

One of God's angels,
whom was robed in spotless white

Descended from the heavens,
and gently kissed the sleeping night

The ebony Goddess arose,
and radiantly transcended away

Leaving behind her illuminating essence,
which the world proclaimed as,
The Dawn of Day

<u>Sunset...</u>

As the hours elapsed,
and the day came to an end

Enclosed in the summers breeze,
a cool chill came within the wind

Dark clouds seemed to seize the earth,
as the sun gradually descended from sight

And though dusk began to encompass the day,
it was not yet considered as night

For amongst the distant horizon,
the sun and the earth intimately met

Surrendering the days final reflections,
which the world proclaimed as,
The Moment of Sunset

Goodnight Granny...

It seemed only as yesterday, even though thirty-plus years have since elapsed from the day I stood beside my grandmother Adell while she laid almost lifeless in Wilson Memorials Hospital bed.

I remember looking up into her eyes, only to see the yellowish tint of death glaring back at me.

"It's time for grandma to go on back home baby", she silently told me as I read the look within her teary eyes. She continued to tell me that her soul was at peace, because serenity had finally come.

I really didn't understand exactly what it was that she was saying to me, but if it was well with her, then it was also well with me. As we continued to stare into each others eyes, we silently conversed without ever uttering a single word.

Although many minutes had quietly faded away, neither of our eyes blinked, never once taking an intermission within our private conversation.

Her gleaming eyes told me not to be afraid, because death was inevitable, and not to be a time of sorrow, but yet a time of rejoicing. She explained to me how she had lived every second of her life awaiting this very moment, and awaiting to hear Gods voice say unto her, "Well done my good and faithful servant".

She went on to explain to me how the devil had plagued her body with cancer, and even though the doctors could do nothing, she was at peace because she knew that God would soon heal her mind, body, and soul from it all.

"But why do you have to leave us?", my young eyes asked as they began to fill with tears.

"My job here is done my beloved grandson", she silently replied, "God is calling me, and now it's time for me to go on back home from which I came", she continued to say without saying.

Though I was only eight years old at the time,

I could comprehend that she wasn't talking about coming back home to grandads' house with me, but instead, she was speaking of going on home to that mansion in heaven which she always prayed about, to be with God.

As I stood there continuing to stare in my grandmothers sleepy eyes, a serene spirit fell over me, as a smile came across grandma's face, assuring me that everything would be alright.

I reached up to take a hold of her hand, and just as I did, I could hear my aunt, whom was standing on the other side of the bed, begin to cry. As I gently caressed grandma's frigid hand, my young eyes gazed around the room watching the tears that slowly flowed from my aunts eyes form a wave that would eventually flow down the faces of everyone that occupied the space of that small room.

As my eyes continued to survey the room, I pondered the reason of why it was that everyone was crying and not smiling, but I guess that grandma didn't tell them what she had silently told me.

"Grandma is napping now", I told my surrounding family the moment I seen her eyes close. I could hear everyone beginning to cry even harder than before, though at that moment, it seemed as if I stood alone with grandma and watched her sleep peacefully despite the pain which the cancer had plagued her body with.

Out of the corner of my eye, I could see that the little red line that had jumped up and down on the TV screen, suddenly stopped.

Then I noticed that the beeping sound that I use to see how many time I could pat my foot in between beep to beep, got stuck and just continued to make one long beep noise.

As I continued to look at the TV screen, I noticed the numbers dropping one by one, as I could feel the weight of my grandmothers hand increase within mine, as her grip quickly vanished.

One by one, people stopped at my grandmothers side to say their final good-byes. It seemed as if the line of people would never end, because by the way it looked, It was like the entire town of Stantonsburg had come out and brought what seemed to be every flower that the earth had ever grown.

I began to wonder just how many people had my grandma Adell known, because never in my life had I seen so many folks in one place at the same time.

After what felt like hours on end, it had finally come time for me and my family to go up and see my grandma. I stood on my tip-toes just so I could see inside of her casket, and as I looked at her, I silently said to her, "See you when I come home grandma", and that's when I heard her voice say back unto me, "I'll be patiently waiting, see you when you get here".

As others cried, I smiled as we walked out of the door of the church into the freezing cold to get back into the long black limo which would take us to my grandmothers final earthly resting place.

As the years passed, I have often reminisced on the yester-years that I use to spend with my grandmother during our short time together.

Visions would begin to be projected in my mind in slow motion of the times grandma would pop me on top of my head with a comb just to get my undivided attention.

I would begin to somewhat laugh as I thought about how my grandmother use to rub her knuckles back and forth across my head until I would surrender to her demands.

Thinking back, I remember that my grandmother never really had to beat me as a child, but when she would, she would make me go out into the yard and get a switch from a bush. And if I picked the smallest switch I could find, she would go back outside and pick the biggest switch she could find. And if she couldn't find one that was big enough to satisfy her, she would then take two or three switches and weave them together to make one big switch, and then beat me twice. The first beating would be for being bad, and the second beating would be for picking out the smallest switch and making her get up and go outside to find another one, at least that's what she always use to say before always saying, "Baby this is gonna hurt me more than it will ever hurt you". I never understood why she use to say that, especially when I was the only one of the two of us whom always walked away crying.

Though thirty-one years have since passed from the time of my grandmothers death, I often find myself reminiscing on what seemed to be only as the moments of yesterday.

"I'll see you when I get there", my heart said to her as I closed my heavy eyes for another nights rest.

My mind would begin to slowly drift into what appeared to be a dream which was to good to be true, for I remembered that I had left the bathroom window open which was right in front of my bedroom door, so when the door crack open, I just blamed it on the wind that blew in from outside.

I also knew that it had been cold outside since the sun had fallen from the sky, so when a cold chill ran over my body, I just blamed it on the cool breeze that drifted in through my bathroom window.

Startled by what resembled a figure in the mist of the shadows, I glanced up only to find nothing, so therefore I blamed it on the moonlight which reflected off of the tree that stood right outside of my bedroom window.

While sleeping, I felt a soft touch on the side of my cheek, and as my reflexes grasped for the culprit, but nothing at all was there, so unconsciously, I blamed it on a fly.

"I'm still waiting, see you when you get here", I dreamed to hear an angelic voice say unto me as I began to feel the corners of my bed getting tight as if someone was tucking me into bed.

Maybe it was all just my imagination, though it all felt to be so real, so when I awoke the next morning, I blamed it all on a dream.

"When Tears Manifest Triumph"

Alone In The Cold...

As the hours passed, and the day came to an end, a young homeless girl stood in front of an small abandoned house wondering if the walls were thick enough to keep the cold wind out. As she continued to further observe the small house from where she stood, she noticed that the old rotten planks in which the house was made of, seemed to serve as solid nourishment for the residential termites which lived there for many years.

It appeared as if she could stand in the front yard of the house, and look right through it into the back yard without ever squinting. Her senses alarmed her, but the oncoming of could rain quickly washed away whatever doubt she may have had of not staying there through the night. Knowing that she had nowhere else to go, she let out a deep sigh and began walking toward the house that would serve as her rest haven for the night. As she took her first step onto the porch of the house, she could feel the boards giving way beneath her feet. The only justification that her young mind could find within the situation was that she only weighed a little over a hundred pounds soaking wet, so therefore, she still felt it would be safe enough for her to continue on. As she placed all of her weight onto the porch, the boards beneath her began to crack and bend, but never did they break.

Walking slowly and cautiously, she made her way through the decayed wooden front door that seemed as if it would fall off of its hinges at any moment. Once inside, she stooped and closely investigated her surroundings, only to find that the house was cluttered with junk and trash which nearly covered the floor. Her young eyes continued to survey the house as she began slowly walking towards what seemed to be a small bedroom. Raking trash out of her way with her foot, she somewhat made a path from the front door to the door of the bedroom. Now standing within the doorway of the bedroom, her gazing eyes danced around, falling on the broken window where the swift breeze of cold wind and rain came through, and then on a old box spring and mattress that sat in the corner of the room, that had been left behind by whoever use to live there.

The more she pondered on the sight of the room, the more her young mind began to wonder if the house was still being used by some crackheads from time to time. She thought to herself that maybe the old box spring and mattress had been brought in by some local addicts from the neighborhood that used the house regularly as a crackhouse.

Her young mind would go back and forth for minutes contemplating if it would be safe for her to stay there through the night because of the possibility of somebody coming back to the house during the night. As she weighed her options, she came to the conclusion that she really had no choice but to stay still through the coming storm. Curious about the rest of the house, she left the tiny bedroom and cautiously surveyed the other two rooms, which was nothing more than a small living room, and a even smaller kitchen area. While looking around in the kitchen, she began searching the few cabinets for any canned foods that may have been left behind or brought in by the crackheads that seem to use the house from time to time.

After opening all of the cabinets doors, the only thing that she could find was the rat balls that had been left behind by the residential rodents. Slamming to doors in frustration, she stormed out of the kitchen to see what she could find in the living room.

As she entered back into the living room, her gazing eyes noticed what seemed to be a picture frame laying on the floor under some trash on the other side of the room. Carefully making her way through the clutter to the picture frame, she reached down and picked up the broken picture frame and shook off the shattered glass, only to find a water damaged picture of what seemed to be a family consisting of a mother and father, along with their two young sons.

While continuing to stare at the degenerated picture, she began to see herself, along with her mother and father within the broken glass of the frame. Instantly, tears began to run down her golden bronze cheeks as she thought about the days she once felt so safe and secure knowing that she would always be protected by her father, and would never be alone because of her mother. "Those were the Days," she mumbled as she began to make her way back to the tiny bedroom.

Still holding the picture in her hand, she flopped down on the old mattress as if the thought of her yester-years had taken all of the life out of her. For moments she just laid there staring at the ceiling while tears continued to run from the corners of her eyes. Her mind began to slowly drift until her thoughts were interrupted by a breeze of cold air.

"Dang, it feels like it's colder in here, than it was outside" she spoke out loud as the cold wind that came through the shattered window on the other side of the room seemed to get even colder.

Holding herself to stay warm, she tried to mentally block out the cold by thinking of her mother who had always told her that overcoming hard times was just a matter of mind over matter, "cause if you don't mind, then it don't matter" she said out loud thinking of how she and her mom used to say that part in unison. "It wouldn't be this way if my mommy and daddy was here" she said to herself while looking at the picture, as tears continued to run slowly down her face. With the thought of her parents still running through her mind, she slowly cried herself to sleep.

After being asleep for an hour or so, the pain of hunger began to overcome her air filled stomach. Awakening to the loud rumbling sounds of her empty belly, she slowly sat up while searching around for the only possession that she still had in the world, which was a navy blue east-pack book bay that her mother had given her at the beginning of the school year, the year before.

She unzipped the book bag and stuck her frail hand inside searching through the open candy bar wrappers and crumbs until she felt half of a snickers bar that she had stolen from the convenient store earlier that day. As she began to nibble on what was left of the half eaten candy bar, she reached back into her book bag and pulled out a red notebook with "Poetic Prayers" written at the top of the front cover. She then unzipped the small pouch on the front of her bag and took out a pen from it.

While her tears once again began to slowly flow down her golden bronze face, thoughts and words began to flow from out of her pen onto the paper in her notebook.

God why has the world turned its back on me,
and left me here in this abandoned house all alone

And why did mommy and daddy leave me so soon,
cause Lord you know I can't make it on my own

God I'm reaching out to you,
and I pray that you will take hold of my hand

God I'm asking you for knowledge and wisdom,
so that I may one day comprehend the things
that I can't now seem understand

God when will you ever calm these storms,
that constantly continues to keep raging in my life

God when will you ever mend my broken heart,
or take me away from all of this struggling and strife

God When?

While writing she began to get drowsy. "You gotta
get some sleep baby girl, cause you got a long day
ahead of you tomorrow" she thought, "I'll finish this

later" she said out loud as she placed her notebook and pen back into her book bag.

"God it's cold in here" she said as she wrapped her arms around herself tighter to keep warm while she began to drift back off to sleep. While sleeping, she tossed and turned as the visions that she saw in slow motion within her dream realistic to her. She was visualizing vivid images of a little girl walking down the street alone; looking for someone to love, and anyone to love her, but no one was in sight.

The little girl within her dream screamed out loud, but it was on one around to hear her silent cry. It was as if she just stood there on the same street, watching the little girl walked right out of her sight. Even though she couldn't see the little girl anymore, she still felt the connection between the two of them.

"God why did you let that man kill my mommy and daddy," she said out loud while still sleeping. "What am I suppose to do now" she continued to say as she tossed and turned until the break of dawn.

As the sun began to rise in the early dawn, Sunlight began to shine through the window while reflecting off of the broken edges of the shattered glass. As her eyes opened to the glare of the sunlight, she swung her arm over her face to block out the bright morning light. While she laid there gathering her thoughts, she thought about the little girl that she had dreamed about. "Its time to get up baby girl," she said to herself as she sat up and cleared the matter out of her eyes.

Now with the journey that awaited her, she stood up and walked to the other side of the room to look out of the broken window, she realized that her dream has now become reality, and that she was indeed the little girl that had been alone in the cold within her dream. "Maybe that's why I couldn't do anything to help her, because I can't even do anything to help myself," she thought as she walked back across the room to pick up her book bag. "Don't go anywhere, cause I might just need you again," she said to the old box spring and mattress that had held her through the night. "I'm out" she said as she followed the foot trail that she had made, from the bedroom towards the front door.

"I almost forgot," she thought as she made he way back into the bedroom to pick up the broken picture frame that she had left beside the mattress. "I got to put you back where you belong" she spoke to towards the family in the picture as she walked back into the living room to find a place to put the picture frame. She saw what seemed to have been used as a TV stand, "this will be a good place," she thought as she put the picture on the little dresser and propped it against the wall. "OK, now I'm out" and walked out onto the porch. "So where do we go from here baby girl" she mumbled to herself under her breath. She looked down the street both ways as she zipped up her coat wondering which way would be the right way for her to go.

"The right way, gotta be the right way," she said to herself as she turned to the right of her, and walked off of the porch and began walking down the street with her book bag on her back and food on her mind, alone in the cold.

<u>The Reunion...</u>

My Mother is nevermore,
as My Father has never been

My Me~Ma is slowly packing her bags,
as My Grandpa is standing at the pearly gates,
eagerly awaiting to be let in

My Uncles are patiently waiting,
as My Grandma prepares a plate for one more

They all screamed "Welcome Home!",
as their kindred spirit came through heavens door

Unconsciously Coherent...

The Sun is brightly shining,
but I can't seem to feel its' rays

The Time is continuously proceeding,
but I feel as if I'm trapped within endless days

My Heart is steadily beating,
but my thoughts pulsate,
to the beat of a different drum

For I find myself spiritually reverting,
back to the unconscious state,
of which I have come

<u>Breaking the Deterred Cycle...</u>

I find myself looking at myself within the reflection of the mirror, but not into the eyes of myself, but yet into the eyes of my unborn son.

My vision begins to blur as his eyes begin to fill with tears while silently asking me, "Daddy will you stop this consistent cycle of crime and imprisonment before I come?"

I lean closer to the mirror and wipe away the steam, intensely searching for the eyes of my daddy and my daddies' daddy, only to ask them if they knew that me and my son would indeed be cursed for the sins of our fathers.

Looking back at me with guilt, they allowed me to know and understand that it was up to me to break the cycle which has plagued our lineage for seven generations, going back to the gangster days of my great-great grandfathers grandfather.

Through my peripheral vision, my mind gazed all the aspects of our lives, desperately looking for a better path for my son to follow, one that has been beaten down by the righteous principles of truth, loyalty, and faithfulness.

Reflecting on the delusive reflections of what appeared to be a life of honor within an unmethodical world full of scorn and contempt, I realized That a change had to come, and the change in which was to be had to start with me.

Detouring my son away from the misguided steps that he may never walk in the shoes of the genealogy of men of which he will come, showing him a brighter path to follow in life, I broke the deterred cycle.

Now that the cycle will be broken for my son to never know, perhaps he'll embrace the love of his family and not that of the streets as I had, becoming the husband in which his wife desires, and the father in which his children need, for it is Gods will.

Maybe he will be the change in which *Sam Cooke* sung of, the Obama of his day, and the hope in which many dream upon, thus allowing him to be recognized as all other great black men such as Malcolm, Marcus, and Martin.

Perchance he will be as the sun in the mid of night, and shelter in the flood of rain, illuminating a way for lost souls to find heavens safe haven, while embracing the minds of the mentally anguished.

Possibly he will become a learned man of self, leading and teaching not only those of his lineage, but also that of the sons and daughters of all, the sagacious ways of the wise.

An aristocrat shall he be, honored by many and respected by all, for he shall emulate the attributes of that of a king as which the blood of royalty flows through his veins.

For by decree he shall become the man which his father has never been, being the righteous man which God has surely destined him to be, because for him, the deterred cycle has been broken.

A Fathers Plea...

I surveyed his every track through the transit of my young eyes, while at times, his staggering stride caused my palliative perception to be in need of adjustment.

Longing to walk in his footsteps, I too found myself stumbling from not being strong enough to lug the heavy load of the massive work boots in which seemed to be made for a giant.

My battered knees ached just as my algetic heart, for I had now realized the possibility of never fulfilling my fathers shoes, for I truly desired to be just as him, for he was my hero.

While my father slept, I laid upon his chest mimicking the pulsations of his heart beat. Often times I would stagger my breath, attempting to synchronize our respiring rhythms to be as one. The entire night through, I would rest placidly within the hammock-like safety net of my fathers arms, for he was indeed my comforter.

As the years elapsed, I would grow even closer to the man whom I viewed as an older reflection of myself. When asked what sounded as an rhetorical question, I could think of no other person other than my father, for he was truly my best friend in the whole wide world.

In time, fathers day became even more important to me than the combination of Thanksgiving and Christmas, and no matter how much I tried to give back unto him of that in which he had given unto me in life, I would always find myself falling short. No words could ever be conjured that could describe the love and support that I felt from him.

Growing up, my mother told me stories of how she and my father began dating in college. I remember her telling me that at the time, my father was a young football star whom critics proclaimed to be a shoo-in for the NFL, but yet he deferred his dreams to care for me and her during his junior year of college. The story of his sacrifice had always stayed etched into my heart since my mother had first told me, so as I wore his number while following in his football cleats, the sound of his voice alone filled me with an sensation as if thousands cheered my name in unison under the roof of a domed stadium.

It was if the sun had fallen from the heavens and fell into a seat at my college graduation, for his exultant smile filled the auditorium as I walked across the stage of my mothers alma mater, garmented in the colors in which he once wore. He didn't have to tell me that he was proud of me, for his facial expression narrated his thoughts as his tears washed away any doubts that I may have had.

Tears flooded my heart with pain as I held my fathers hand within mine while watching my son lay upon his chest as I had when I was just a child as him. Reminiscing, I once again staggered my breath attempting to breathe in unison with the respirator that was now keeping my father alive. Though all the impossible dreams that I've dreamed within my life, I never imagined the possibility of my fathers death, for even within reality, he was immortal, thus his radiance would forever be remembered.

The soil from which he came slowly fell from my hand, raining upon his coffin, showering him with my respects of love and honor. The inevitable appeared unbelievable, causing me to stumble from the emotional quakes that mentally trembled my earthly foundation. I then realized that it was because of all the burdens in which my father once carried upon his shoulders that caused him to stumble at times, but yet and still, no matter how much he stumbled, he never fell as I did when I attempted to lug around his heavy work boots as a child. I remember him telling me that I was not yet strong enough to carry his load, meaning that it was not yet time for me to walk in his shoes, but that there would come a day in which I would indeed have to fill his shoes and walk in a straighter line than he had in life, and that day was now today for me, for now I am my sons father.

"When Expression Feels Like Ecstacy"

Coitally Kidnapped...

Enslaved by the sadistic inflictions of his perversive thoughts, chastely tears of blood untimeously menstruated through the genital orifice of her pristine being as she silently cried from within.

Her bellowing sighs suffocated the serenity within the nights air, compelling the coital intruder to muffle her sobbing pleas within the forceful grasp of his hand.

"Shut up!", he aggressively uttered as he continued to strip the celestial tree of it's unripe fruits, kidnapping her of her precious innocence.

"God please help me, I need you!", she desperately mumbled beneath her gasping breath, just hoping that at least God would hear her silent cry for protection, even if no one else would.

The Abyss...

The Darkness
refused to release its grasp of me,
as I struggled to escape the cousin of death

Vivid images
encompassed my subconscious thoughts,
as I gasped for air,
while being deprived of breath

The dew of fear drenched my slumber corpus,
as I frantically fought to stay alive

Clawing and scratching through the dirt of the dark,
refusing to accept the thought of being buried alive

Scrambling to find a break of daylight,
while trying to break free of this achromatic disguise

Tossing and turning as I endured the struggle,
while anxiously awaiting the moment ,
I would awake and open my eyes

<u>Til' Death Did Us Part...</u>

He was all I've ever known, my everything, my humongous safety net beneath my unstable trapeze wire of a life, just as he was my personal size hammock in the back yard beneath well shaded trees on a hot summers day. I loved him more than life itself, for I knew he felt the same way of me, even though many attempted to convince me otherwise.

"You're becoming second in his life, why can't you realize it?", my mother and sister would argue, proclaiming that I was no longer his first love.

I would admit that we had our problems, but nothing that I truly didn't believe time would eventually solve. I could see it in his eyes that he needed me now more than ever, therefor I felt that it was up to me to provide a soft shoulder to comfort him after his long hard days at work.

Each day I patiently awaited for him to return home from work with a hot meal, his bathing water prepared, and my will to do whatever it took to comfort him. Daily I awaited to please him with the surety as the rising of the sun.

At first it started off as I had planned, but then shortly thereafter, the hot meals became cold, the bathing water would go unused, and my comforting endeavors seemed to be no longer desired. With each night that passed, he began to arrive home at later times, ignorantly walking through the door and straight to bed. It then became clear to me that his mysterious affair was in the process of destroying our marriage.

My heart crumbled as the words of my mother and sister slowly became reality. I knew something had to be said, though I didn't know what should be said, or how to say it. All I could do was sit and ponder on the thoughts which seized my serenity.

Normally I would have already gone to bed and cried myself to sleep. But not tonight. Tonight was the night, we had to talk.

The clock struck a quarter~pass~midnight when he staggered in the door heading towards the bedroom.

"Move out of my way" He aggressively screamed back at me, pushing me through the door and onto the floor beside the bed. I hastily jump up off of the floor, only to be struck back down by the thrust of his heavy hand.

Tears fell simultaneously along with my heart in which had seemed to fall into the pit of my stomach and shattered. My mind intensely researched the physical encounterances of our past, but none came to mind, for never has he hit me before.

" I love him, and he loves me" I compulsively told my mother and sister as the years elapsed, while more of trying to convince myself.

"No one that loves you, Physically hurts you"
They continued to argue, as their truthful words
fell upon deaf ears during their seemingly cross
examination.

I was the judge and jury during this trial of mine,
and from neither side could I find any fault in the
man I loved so much. In all actually, I found more
fault in myself than I ever have in him. For to me, it
was I who denied him when he needed me ,   thus
causing him to fall into the temptation of drinking to
find comfort, rather than in me, his wife.

It was also my fault that I outraged him to the
point of striking me, something that he promised me
he would never do, I guess I should have let him be.
It was all my fault, so therefore, I felt that it was up to
me to fix the problems that I caused.

"You need to leave him", they pleaded to me with
all sincerity.

"But he needs me" I proclaimed, determined to
do whatever it took, for I truly loved him to death.

I vowed to love him and to never forsake him until death did us part, but never did I imagine that the face of death would be identical as his.

I cried for the help of God as his heavy right hand came crashing down upon my sensitive face.

"Please stop! Please!" I continuously pleaded from the depth of my soul. Physically and emotionally I felt as if my heart was being ripped right out of my being.

"But why?" I unconsciously continued to cry out loud within my soul until the sound of my pleading voice whispered into the ears of God, for suddenly within my mist of torment, came serenity, for death had finally done us part.

And even now, after the twelve long years that I've been in this prison, my heart still loves him just as it did the day we got married. But why should I be punished because I love me more?

<u>Reparations...</u>

I have...

Restless Nights,
endued by renewed mental fights

Candid Thoughts,
of unresolved plights

Questions without Answers,
as my mind tosses and turns

Conscious Nightmares,
as my soul constantly burns

For This...
Is my Reparations of Remorse

<u>If only...</u>

If life was to be forever lived,
then surely, death would have never been

And if the omega
was destined to precede the alpha,
then spiritual righteousness
could never exist without sin

So I ask,
could it be true that God is indeed
the Devils advocate?

for if it is true that
the presence of God is omnious,
then where doesn't thoust dwell?

for if the omnipresence of God
is within all existence,
then surely, God must also reside in hell

Thus causing darkness to be lifes cosmical yen,
with light being its complementary yang

For out of darkness came spiritual manifestation,
thus causing the spheric trinity
to be as one of the same

Hence proclaiming God alone as omnificent,
for there is no other that is unlimited
in his creative worth

For it is written,
that God simply spoke it and it was,
and from within the same breathe
came Heaven, Hell, and Earth

So I ask,
could it also be true that the Devil
is indeed Gods advocate?

The Conspiracy Theory...

I stood alone awaiting the final fate of my destiny for the sins I would be judged upon, for the time has now come.

Quietly, the judicial majesty sat upon his throne as the arbitrator of my deeds in life, portraying the presence of God, though the robe in which he was garmented, completely contradicted the attributes of innocence.

Echoes of vague voices seized my serenity, as confusion and anxiety conquered my omniscient optimism.

My heart fell simultaneously with the gavel, shattering as if it laid beneath the mallet in which the judge pounded against his wooden bench, for this sort of knocking on wood wouldn't indicate a figurative gesture of good luck for me.

"Will the defendant Rise?", the bailiff requested, seeming as if he was ordering me to stand in the center of a ten man firing squad.

"Guilty!", the judges verdict rung out through the court room as gunfire within the silence of the midnight air.

The U.S. Marshall apprehended my apprehension as the tightening clicks of the cuffs in which he placed upon me resonated reality, for when my teary eyes opened, I found the limbs of my grandmother and brother chained to mine, for they also had been charged with conspiracy.

"Why them!", my soul cried.

"Why must they also suffer for my sins!", I repeatedly appealed to no avail.

Inevitably, unwarranted indictments would in time affect all of whom cared for me, especially that of my ex-girlfriend, for she sacrificed the freedoms of her heart, only to be bound by the shackles of love.

Throughout the time I spent in prison, her love for me incarcerated her also, at least four hours every two weeks, because just as me, she was also subjected to strip searches, dress codes, time limits, and every other rule and regulation enforced by the bureau of prisons under the observant eyes of its guardsmen.

Wonderment penetrated my thoughts as I pondered the question of whether it was her whom was locked in, or was it me whom was locked out, for at times, prison and society seemed to be as if one of the same.

"Why them!", my soul once again cried nightly.

"Why must they also suffer for my sins!", I appealed my verbal affidavit to the ears of God, for I knew with assurance that the only conspiracy in which my loved ones were guilty of, was that of conspiring to unconditionally love and support a sinner such as me.

Growing Pains...

Silent prayers comfort my contrite soul,
as sincere words heal my bleeding ears

Extended arms mends my broken heart,
as gentle touches ease my greatest fears

Loyalty calms my agony,
as compassionate actions dry my falling tears

Reality has served as my motivation,
as faith has allowed me to persevere
through the many years

Knowledge has stimulated my mind,
as comprehension has defined
my struggles and strife

Words of wisdom have opened my 3rd eye,
as understanding has illuminated my life

The Holy Hour...

Dust of crumbling rock transformed the day into night as clouds of nightmares engulfed the conscious dreams of lady liberty.

Her soul burned with insecurity, exposing her camouflaged vulnerability as smoke signals revealed the truth of her to the world.

Plagued with an evil epidemic, her tainted blood affected all of whom took part in her immoral acts of harlotry.

Though once esteemed as a lady of monetary merit, the beguiling disease which encompassed her being caused her to become just as worthless as the debris which laid beneath her feet.

"Come out of her", the silent voice within their righteous hearts told them as they scurried to escape miscarriage through the womb of her Babylonian belly.

Thus innocent souls abandoned their existence, attempting to flee the wrath of her destined destruction as the world witnessed her hour of judgement.

As Death Becomes Me...

Death becomes me,
as the Ink begins to dry

Thus my life becomes numb,
for my soul can no longer cry

Death becomes me,
as I grasp my bleeding pen in hand

Smearing my last words upon pages,
which only God could understand

Death becomes me,
as the Ink gradually fades

Depriving me of spiritual resolutions,
forever leaving my soul dismayed

Thus death becomes me,
as the Ink begins to dry

For I live through my pen,
and without life, I must die

Thus Death Becomes Me

<u>Be It Beautiful...</u>

Oh what a beautiful struggle it is,
to live in so much pain and anguish,
and still prevail

What a beautiful journey it is,
to walk into heaven,
after spending your entire life in hell

Oh how beautiful of a romance it must be,
to find the love of God,
within an earthly angel such as your wife

And how beautiful it is to feel,
when you embrace the feeling of a beautiful life

Oh how Beautiful...

<u>Destined...</u>

My destiny has been blessed to me,
therefore it is what it is

My life has been a lesson learned,
therefore even within defeat, I still win

My voice has been my poetry,
and my life has been my song

Darkness has been my safe haven,
while learning self has been my resurrection

Suffering has been my motivation,
while perseverance has been my strive to perfection

Day and Night no longer seems to be real anymore,
for my dreams have now become reality

Even Life and Death seem as one and the same,
for through my words, I'll exist eternally

For This Is My Destiny...

<u>Trapped in the Abyss...</u>

Through the desolate years of my life, my dry tears have left impressions on my face in the form of fossilized tattoos.

My brown eyes have become hazel from me constantly shedding tears, while reminiscing on the struggles of my past life blues.

My tender heart has become frigid due to being unprotected from the harshness of cold nights and hail-stoned rain.

My profound thoughts have become migraines due to the overwhelment of my lifes heart aches and perpetual pains.

My perception of self has become distorted due to the misunderstanding of the lineage of which I am from.

My sweet dreams have now become nightmares due to me opening my eyes and realizing what it is that my life has become.

For I Am A Poetic Prisoner...

For it is Written...

My poetic concinnity mentally conquers my enemy
via the verbal syntax of my lifes philosophy

Having to accept the reality of my families history,
while dissecting the reason for eternal misery

Understanding that my wretched young history is
not the determination of the actuality of my destiny

For it is written
within the sacred scriptures of my poetic prophecy,
but yet you say that my testimony
is nothing more than a hypocrisy

So therefore,
I patiently expect death at any given time,
for I spiritually understand
that my life is not that of mine

For death is not a possibility, rather a given
for we are born with death being
the inevitable completion of living

"When Love Nolonger Begets Lust"

Addicted...

The thought of him persistently antagonizes me, mirroring my sweet dreams in the visions of vivid nightmares.

Convulsions awaken my peaceful mind, compelling me to fiend for a chance to slow dance with that ole boy my soul yearns for, that we may mentally embody the melodies of that old song, "Stairway to Heaven".

Longing for a taste of his pleasures, I intensely search for his touch through my blind eyes, desperately attempting to scratch that irrepressible itch which consumes me.

And at last, his bliss engulfs my very essence, massaging my tingling nerves until the point I'm calm enough to once again nod-off into the delightful sweet dreams of my utopian fantasy.

<u>Engagingly Embedded...</u>

The dagger of her piercing words
surpassed the stone walls of my sheltered heart

Engraving mental mirages of ecstasy
in the essential nature of hieroglyphic art

Telepathically connecting with my soul,
visually revealing her essence as being heaven-sent

Spiritually decoding the celestial scriptures,
while teaching me to understand
the sacred decipherment

For She Is My Angel...

<u>Repentantive Reparations...</u>

I offer you reparations of a brighter future
in repayment for our darker past

For I have now grown to learn and understand
that without true love,
nothing is promised to last

For forever will become forbidden,
causing tomorrow to become for-nevermore

Happiness will become obsolete,
causing a kiss to never be
as it was once before

Smiles will become fraudulent,
while saying I Love You,
will become compulsive lies

Holding hands will become an affection of deceit,
while walking step for step
with the devil in disguise

So therefore, I offer you reparations
of a brighter future
in repayment for our darker past

For I have now grown to learn and understand,
that without unconditional love,
nothing will surely last

<u>Sweet Rhapsodia...</u>

Your name is as a melody
whispered within my echoic heart,
spiritually serenading my suffering soul

Thus the psalmody of your silent song
hummed hymns within my thoughts,
spiritually sung to significantly console

The harmony of your harpic voice
resonates throughout the heavens of my mind,
for your songs are synonymous
with that of an angels poetic petition

For the rhapsody of your rhapsodic prayers
has granted my suffering soul
eternal remission

As Time Will Tell...

It has time whom has bonded us together,
and time whom has once torn us apart

Time whom has comforted our contrite souls,
and time whom has healed our broken hearts

Time whom has spiritually nurtured us,
and time whom has allowed us to grow

Time whom has evolved you and I
into the oneness that we both now know

Thus causing us to become
TIMELESS...

<u>Spiritually Eclipsed...</u>

Beloved we are as the sun and the moon, for we are man and woman, husband and wife, two celestial bodies who have been predestined by the creator himself to co-exist interdependently for the procreation of life to be.

Though we are physically separate, we are yet and still as one, being that we both are the light of the world, for when I shine brightly through the day, you illuminate the night with the mere presence of your heavenly being.

My love we were created to complement each other in every meaning of the word. But yet at times just as the sun and the moon, we spiritually eclipse ourselves by obscuring the light of the other from that of which depends upon us the most, for just as the earth and its inhabitants depend upon the sun and the moon for their lights, our children within and beyond depend upon us for our lights of guidance.

So therefore beloved, we are as the sun and the moon, for we are man and woman, husband and wife, two celestial beings who have been predestined by God to co-exist interdependently for the providence of life. So lets not eclipse each other and intercept the world of our essential light.

<u>My First Love...</u>

At times I feel as if I need her, and maybe I don't, but then again, maybe I do.

Cause it was her who has always inspired me and has never left me no matter what I've been through.

It was her who has never lied to me, nor forsaken me at the worst times of my life.

Just as it was her who sat with me faithfully in my prison cell when I was being abandoned by the one that I thought would be my wife.

So therefore, I fell in love with her as if she was my soulmate, cause it was her, and only her, who seemed to love me unconditionally.

For it was her who showed me who truly loved me, and if the truth be told, she even showed me some things about myself I never wanted to see.

And because of all that she has done for me, I dedicate this poem and my life to my new found love, whose name is Loneliness.

A Poets Paradox...

If everything was perfect,
then what would be the need for perfection

Why would ones heart yearn for companionship,
if never knowing the feeling of neglection

What would be the meaning of meaningless,
if everything meant something or another

How would one ever appreciate anything,
without ever experiencing one without the other

What would one even be,
if one only existed to equate as nothing

Thus how could nothing even be defined,
if in valued opinion,
everything existed as something

Therefore, what would the value
of ones opinion even be?

<u>To Be, Or Not To Be…</u> <u>(I Wonder)</u>

I wonder if it's raining from the clouds,
or if the angels of heaven
are simply shedding tears

I wonder if God has blessed me
with the clarity of understanding,
or if these mental mirages
continue to be not what it appears

I wonder if the source of energy
within my timepiece has died,
or if the rotation of the sun and moon
has surely ceased

I wonder if the plague of mental glaucoma
has vagued my vision,
or if it's because of the tears
my eyes have yet released

I wonder while spiritually wandering,
will any answers ever come to erase my doubt

Hence I wonder will God ever bless me
with such clarity that I may understand
what this life is all about

Oh how wonderful it would be,
if it was to ever be...

But I wonder will it ever?

<u>A Lesson Learned...</u>

At times I detested his very presence, for he was as an annoying mosquito who persisted on pinching away at my very last nerve. I had done all that I could to ignore him, but seemingly, the sound of his voice screeched within my thoughts as acrylic fingernails upon a chalkboard.

"What are *you* doing?", he rhetorically asked, seeing me apparently concentrating on the work in which I had before me.

"Not now", I sharply said, knowing that he would understand my requested indication, while trying not to scramble the pieces of thoughts I had formulated within my mind.

"Okay", he said, turning away from me and taking five steps forward before turning back around and asking me with a blank face, "What about now?".

I smiled at him, attempting to disguise the fact that he had now sent my complaisant thoughts racing in the quest of catching my composure.

I looked up at him with my piercing eyes, then back at the incomplete sentence I was working on, restraining the profane words that fought against my lips to be released from the captivity of my oral cavity.

I sat quietly as the decisions of good and evil battled in a game of tug-of-war within my mind. Back and forth, my thoughts struggled for dominant position before yielding to the sound of his voice. I looked back up at him, diverting my question to my-self of why was it that he insisted on bothering me.

"It's hard to be consistent isn't it?", he replied to my silent thoughts.

As his words filtered through my mind, lingering as stratus clouds within the atmosphere, he turned away and slowly disappeared from my sight.

" I guess it is", I said to myself, now realizing his step by step observation of my spiritual walk.

<u>Destiny Manifested...</u>

I am as the man whom they said would never walk again, but because of faith and perseverance, In time became the fastest man on earth.

I am as the child who they said would miscarry, but lived to fight another day despite the complications I faced at birth.

I am as the rose that grew through concrete which has been scratched and torn by lifes trials and tribulations, but still survived against all odds and doubt to prevail.

I am as negative words manifested in prolific poetry, truthfully testifying the distressed emotions of the spiritually despondent, while redirecting lost souls away from hell.

I am as a smutty piece of coal that time and pressure has formed into a flawless diamond, because God has molded and polished me to the point of unpurified perfection.

Just as I am the ugly duckling whom has been transformed into a beautiful swan, because I've been made in the image of Gods reflection

So how could I not be
Gods divine replica of manifest destiny.

<u>Spiritual Warfare...</u>

I have many problems,
but no solutions

No soldiers to stand beside me,
though I fight many revolutions

I hurt through the day,
but no tears will fall at night

I keep my internal emotions concealed,
for I can't show fear in the face of my plight

I can't even show the slightest love,
for the enemy may attack my weakness

I can't even show signs of my strengths,
for I must allure them with my meekness

Therefore I have many problems,
with a mind filled with confusion

No one to help me in this spiritual war,
as I fight these Redemptive Revolutions

A Poets Prophecy...

My understanding heart
has heartfelt tears standing under my eyes

For I now understand,
that my life is written within the sacred scrolls,
only to be fulfilled on the day of my demise

For death will become the alpha,
thus causing the omega to become the beginning

Thus my poetical sacrifice will become infinite,
while detouring the lost souls
of those who are consciously sinning

For just as plainly as it has been written,
the soul that sins shall surely die

Therefore I must poetically intercede for their souls
by sacrificing the blood within my pen
to the most high

For that is my purpose as a Poetic Prophet

The Passion OF THE PEN

"When Hell Appears as Heaven"

American Born....

I am the lost son of Africa,
for she is indeed my estranged mother

Kidnapped and taken before my birth,
thus enslaving me
within the unjust foster care of another

Mentally battered and physically abused,
disconnecting me from my African History

Depriving me of cultural intellect,
forcing my ancestry
to become an African-American Mystery

Alienating me from the origin
of my natural environment,
coercing my free soul into spiritual deprivation

Compelling me to cry out for my unknown mother,
while yearning for the unknown relationship
of my African Nation

The Concrete Jungle <u>(the prose)</u>

Without a trace, his footprints stealthily pursued the alluring game which enticed his hunger for survival.

Discreetly lurking within the shrubbery of the jungles murky shadows, his gazing eyes surveyed the lewd landscape of his nocturnal environment as his keen intuition sensed the precarious aura within the nights air.

Camouflaged within the graffiti of the jungles urine stained turf, his raring eyes prance voraciously insync with the precipitated movements of his chase.

Dashing as a bolt of lightning, he jolts through the night striking his target, repleting his innate appetite for self-preservation.

The taste of success marinates in his mind as he contemplates the provisional victory of surviving another day within the concrete jungle.

<u>The Concrete Jungle</u> <u>(the short story)</u>

On the branches of her third story apartment window, the little gray haired old lady quietly sits and observes the nocturnal environments of her neighborhood.

A cordless phone lies rested in her lap. The ever so often skittering voice of Mahalia Jackson serenades her soul. The pot of boiling water on top of the old gas stove, fragranced with a piece of cinnamon stick, dampens the arid air of her studio styled apartment.

She peacefully hums out of tune with the record, as she nods to every familiar face, and even strangers, that wave as they pass her by.

The youngling of the neighborhood call her "the owl" because of the way she's always sitting up in her window watching everybody and everything that goes-on on the block, not to mention the way she was always yelling out questions in her own community watch sort of way. "Who's car is that?" She would ask, "I never seen that car around here before." Or, "who is he Ty-ty, is he a new friend from school?" or even funny questions like, "who she thank she is wearing that colorful handkerchief wrapped around her butt looking like she should be in one of them Vicki secrets ads, I know she didn't? Respectably so, the older folks in the area called her ma'mae. Mainly because, in her own way, she practically in some way or another raised every child in that neighborhood, even those who may now be forty years old or better. Many she has baby-sitted at some point in time, and others, she just treats as if they are her own.

Some say that she would feed you, preach to you, educate you, and hug you all in the same breath.

In spite of all the chaos and discord within the jungle they called home, all could agree on one thing. Despite the many robberies, murders, and all the other immoral acts that often took place on the 67th block of Elvie street, ma'mae door always stayed safely open, literally and metaphorically, for the community which she has watched over, also always watched over that little gray haired old lady sitting up in her window.

Oh yeah!, did I mention that ole night owl, ma'mae, was legally blind, cause every time the police would come by and ask her about something, she ain't never seen nothing.

Born Tyrone Tyler, Ty-ty was a youthful live wire. The street was his playground, and the games in which he engaged in had no rules. He was slender, yet vigorous. His facial features were that of a model's, and his complexion was dark as the midnight itself. He was roughly elegant, and his natural intellect spawned his street savvy.

Ma'mae had all but given birth to Ty-ty. She was even his mother's midwife at the time he was born.

" I ain't never stop praying for you since the day you was born" she would always tell him, subliminally telling him that she wished he would stop running the streets as he did.

Son of a former Black Panther, Ty-ty was inbreded with the rebellious and revolutionistic ways in which he often displayed. Although he never knew his father, he was fascinated with his fathers life, the stories he often heard about him, and the fact that he was a Black Panther. "I am my fathers son" Ty-ty would often boast, proclaiming that he too was willing to die in the streets, for just as his father, he too was a soulja fighting within the American jungle of the ghetto he called home.

Ty-ty knew everybody, and everybody knew him, even those outside of the boundaries of his proximity. Within the perimeters he was commonly known as a peddler; drugs, guns, you name it, he had it, or at least could get it within a couple of phone calls. To those outside the territorial 67th street, Ty-ty was nothing more than a jack boy.

His prey feared him, and the other predators within the concrete jungle respected him, therefore, always within their second thought, they opted to let him be.

Embodying the characteristics of a black panther, Ty-ty would prowl the streets in search of his prey nightly. Blending in with the shadows of the broken streetlights, he would quietly observe his surroundings, sniffing for the aroma of weakness in some around the way drug dealer.

"Now he knows he's out of pocket", Ty-ty says to himself, watching, JT, a known drug dealer from the eastside of town, make his way into an all night deli on 69th and Attucks ave.

Ty-ty knows that JT is swift as an antelope when it comes to maneuvering his way out of sticky situations, so Ty-ty laid low on him, awaiting the perfect opportunity to strike.

JT comes out of the deli with a bag in one hand, and his cell phone to his ear in the other. He looks around for the sight of anything suspicious as he opens his car door, but without a second glance, ignores his intuition. Seemingly from out of nowhere, Ty-ty dashes out from beneath the murky alley, puts a pistol to JT's head and forces him into his own car.

The next day, JT's car is found abandoned and burned beyond recognition. JT becomes a familiar statistic, as Ty-ty eats well from the gains of his healthy hunt. Knowing how ups can become downs, and how predators can also become prey, Ty-ty decided to share his hunt with his cousin Monty, whom he just always referred to as Famm. Knowing his cousin's position in the streets, Ty-ty thought of his move as something like giving his cousin a retainer just in case he would need his back one day if word ever leaked to the street that he was the one who licked on JT.

Monty was at least a decade older than Ty-ty, and to think of it, biologically, was actually Ty-ty's uncle on his mother's side. Though he respected him as so, Ty-ty never saw Monty as an uncle, more like a a big brother, but being that Monty had always called Ty-ty cuz since his childhood, Ty-ty only responded as he thought accordingly. It was only until Ty-ty got old enough to figure out that Monty always called him cuz because of Monty's gang slang, Crypts called all of their own cuz, but being that Ty-ty has never really been into the gang thang, he stopped calling Monty, cuz, and just referred to his uncle simply as Famm.

Famm was also a pretty-boy in his own right, but unlike Ty-ty, he was short and stocky with a sun-like golden complexion. His burly muscular build made him a natural intimidator and his monarchial mentality made him a born leader. A Crypt by blood; he called himself, for he too was his fathers son. Taking reign as heir to his fathers throne, Famm took pride in being head of his prided herd. Indeed he was the king of the concrete jungle, as tattooed on the entirety of his right shoulder.

Literally speaking, Famm's ambiental nature made him loved by many and respected by all.

In one, he was both dangerous and compassionate, aggressively militant and candidly meek, thuggishly rugged and attractively elegant. Be it often said, "Famm in his own way is a true gangster and a gentleman." Even Ma'mae thought of him to be different from all the other gangsters and bangers in which she had seen run through the streets during her time.

" He's not just another hoodlum out there" she said, "He's the protector of the community, in a since, our very own robin hood in a sort", explaining how that no matter how much wrong he may do, all the good he does for everybody in their community.

Proclaimed as a modern day Huey Newton, Famm was more than just some stereotypical trouble making gang leader as often depicted by the media. Also heavily influenced by the Black Panther party, not to mention his insight from books such as ;"Last man standing" of Geranimo Pratt, or "Blood In My Eye" and " Soledad Brother" by George Jackson, Famm saw a urging need for the revolution of his people. As an avid reader, he was capable of comprehending the scripted political segregation and economical slavery, known as classism, as opposed to the old chapters of blatant racism.

Thought at first glance, the concrete jungle may appear to those looking outside in as a haven of animalistic savagery, for in their eyes, they can only see those who live within; scraping, scheming, scrambling, and even scoundreling to make ends meet. But to those who choose to mentally take a closer look at the miry mirage, they'll see the inveterated cultivation of this erudite civilization.

Even at second thought, many may even come to the conclusion that the concrete jungle isn't in anyway different from any other community, for we all in some shape, form, or fashion, have lurking around us the likeness of an old con artist such as Jake the snake disguised in his cunning deceptive demeanor. Or even the likens of hecklers harassing the timid in the way of the hyenas of the African dusk-lands.

So whether it be the well dressed crabs in a bucket trampling the others in their path to the top of the corporate ladder, or be it, the panhandler's mooching for pocket change on the corners of the store fronted streets, as the ambiental appearance of the sun and moon continues to revolve, so does life within the concrete jungle.

For the Red, White, and Blue...

At the age of seven, he pulled his first trigger. At the age of ten, he hit his first target. And now at the age of thirteen, he is considered as one of the most well trained child prodigies in America. Though he was born as every other ordinary child, he was everything but raised to be like any other ordinary kid.

His glaring eyes give off the reflection of cold steel, seeming as if they could pierce directly through a persons soul.

His jet-black hair blends in with the night, as his impassive appearance wears a look that could intimidate the heart of a killer.

His parents are listed as non-existent, his next of kin are unknown, and his lineage is untraceable.

Some call him a soldier, while others called him a mercenary, but whatever the case may be, he was born to kill and die for his gang.

<u>Detached...</u>

"911, How may I help you?", A ladies voice echoed through the phone, attempting to calm the panicked breaths that accosted her via the emergency switch board.

"My family is missing", a mans voice intermittently answered, "One minute they were here, and the next, they were gone", the frantic voice of the seemingly distraught man continued to say as he paced back and forth, only taking two to three steps at a time in each direction.

"Please calm down sir and tell me what happened", the operator requested to no avail, being interrupted before she could complete her scripted sentences.

"Don't you tell me to calm down lady, you just get somebody over here right now", the man aggressively responded to her obvious prototypical petition, "I'm at 721 Hollow Falls Court, and I expect someone to be here shortly" he continued, still rapidly pacing back and forth in front of the place where he had just seen his family.

"Sir someone is on the way as we speak, and I understand that you are upset sir, but I need for you to explain to me exactly what happened, and when was it that you realized that your family was missing" the operator inquired, attempting to withdraw more information from the hysterical man than he was willingly offering to give.

"Where are they?", the mans crackling voice desperately questioned just before catching a glimpse of a unmarked navy-blue cop car pulling into his driveway.

"They're here", he said more to himself than the operator as he disconnected their phone conversation while approaching the cop car.

The door popped open as the long legs of the slender agent slowly exited his patrol car.

"Thank you for coming" the man greeted the agent before the car door could close behind him.

"Agent Lewis, and you are?", the agent inquired of the man within his breif introduction.

"I'm Danny Watkins sir, the one whom called concerning my missing family", Mr. Watkins replied in a calmer than normal manner.

"Please tell me what happened sir"

"Well basically Agent Lewis, myself along with my wife and kids were in the car getting ready to pull off to Emerald Point when my wife realized that she forgot our youngest sons medicine bag in the house. So I jumped out of the car, ran into the house and grabbed the bag, and when I came back outside, they were gone".

"So how long were you gone?", the agent asked, opening the door to the house, allowing Mr. Watkins to enter inside first.

"Only a matter of seconds, no more than a minute. I dashed in, and right back out, so literally speaking sir, one minute they were here, and the next minute they were gone".

The agent began to explore the house room by room, looking for anything out of the ordinary that may cause a concern for any foul play.

"Do you have any enemies that you can think of right off hand Mr. Watkins?".

"No sir, not at all", he answered with a mixture of asurity and confusion.

"What about your relationship with your wife, have you and her had any problems recently that would cause her to want to leave you?".

"Of course not, what are you trying to imply agent Lewis?", sensing the feeling as if he was morphing from victim to suspect.

As the agent took into his hand a picture frame that laid upon Mr. Watkins' entertainment center, Mr. Watkins stepped up beside Agent Lewis and began a formal introduction of his family.

"This is when we were at the beach for my baby girls' birthday", Mr. Watkins began to say, dragging his pointer finger across the the picture in a reminis-cent manner, "I've always loved taking pictures of my family, the only problem is, I just never get a chance to be in the picture myself", Mr. Watkins continued to tell Agent Lewis, taking the picture frame out of the agents hand, and gazing at the photo as if he could still feel the cool breeze off the ocean on that exact hot summer day.

"May I take a look at your sons medicine bag Mr. Watkins?", the agent curiously asked, as the fragmented pieces to the mysterious puzzle began falling into place all by their self.

<u>Chemistry 151...</u>

<u>-May 7th-</u>

"Close the door behind you Chris", Bradley told his roommate as the two young men made their way down the steps into their basement.

"Are you sure you know what you're doing man?", Chris asked as he turned on the black light hanging over an old dusty kitchen table.

"I told you my dad use to be a chemist, so I'm sure that the apple didn't fall far from the tree", Brad replied as he began to take the supplies needed for the experiment out of a box that he had pulled from beneath the table.

"You got everything you need?" Chris curiously questioned while gazing over the stuff Brad began placing on the table.

"I got all that I need for now, I won't need the rest of it until later", Brad said, opening a whole loaf of ryebread and putting it into a bread pan.

"Hey, open just one of those bottles", Brad told Chris as he finished poking holes through the shell on top of the ryebread.

"Are you going to pour that whole bottle in there?", Chris asked, closely observing everything his friend was doing.

"Yeah, it has to soak through all of the bread, this is what causes the fermentation process, that's why it has to be 190% Proof", the young self-proclaimed chemist explained to his friend as he put the bread-pan inside of the broken refrigerator he once used in college.

"Well Chris, that's it for now, the process has began".

"So how long do we wait now?", Chris asked as he cut off the black light, and turned to follow Brad back up the basement stairs into the house.

"Fourteen days my friend, just fourteen days", Brad answered, holding the door open looking back into the basement as he was looking into the future.

<u>-May 21st-</u>

The basement door cracked open as the boys made their way back down into the lab to begin the second stage of their experiment.

After getting everything situated, Brad walked over to the old refrigerator to retrieve the bread pan.

"Hold your breath, cause it's not gonna be a pleasant smell", Brad said as he placed his hand on the handle and opened the door.

"Damn-it man, it smells like it's a dead body in there", Chris exclaimed as the hideous stench penetrated through his face mask, piercing his nostrils.

"That's why I told you to hold your nose, cause I knew it was gonna stink like hell, cause trust me, that's the one thing that I remeber clear as day about this whole process when my dad used to do it", Brad laughingly said to his roommate while reading the disgusted look on his face.

Brad placed the bread pan on top of the work

table and began to knock off the top layer of the bread. Then he poured the other unused bottle of alcohol, just as he had done he first bottle fourteen days earlier.

"Well my friend, back into the fridge you go", Brad said to himself as if he was speaking to the bread pan.

"Are you ready Professor Wilson?", Brad sarcastically said to Chris because of the way he never did anything to help him, but always carefully observed his every move.

"So how much longer now?", Chris asked without responding to the rhetorical question that Brad had just asked him.

"Just one day longer than the last time", Brad replied as him and Chris made their way back up the steps and through the basement door.

-June 5th-

Chris walked into the house and looked at his roommate sitting on the couch watching a movie.

"Are you ready Dr. Jekyll?", Chris inquired as he made his way to the kitchen with bags in hand.

"So did you get everything?", Brad asked as he jumped up off the couch and made his way into the kitchen stride for stride right behind Chris.

"I think so, you tell me since you're the chemical genius", Chris replied, unloading the bags onto the kithen table as if he was scattering out small pieces to a puzzle.

"Alrighty then buddy, let's see what you got here", Brad teased as his eyes slowly scanned the kitchen table for all of the needed necesities to complete their chemical experiment.

"It looks like you did good my friend, at least you're good for something", Brad said as he pulled his list of supplies out of his pocket so they could check it off to make sure they had everything they needed to complete their project.

"You call it, and I'll check it off", Brad told Chris as they took a seat on opposite sides of the table.

"OK now, we got two packs of tweezers, a jug of purified water, two packs of black construction paper, a box of plastic reynolds wrap, two jars of gerber baby food, a two inch deep oven pan, a bottle of visine eye drop for the eye droppers, and last but not least, the preforated galaxy sticker paper", Brad called out as Chris checked off the supply list.

"Looks like you did well buddy, so lets take all this stuff down stairs and put it away for Saturday, and make sure you get some good sleep tomorrow night, cause Saturday will be a very long day for us", Brad informed his scientific sidekick as the two gathered up all of their supplies and stored them away awaiting their next work day.

"How long is very long?", Chris curiously asked.

"At least fifteen to sixteen hours or so, just depending if everything goes according to plan and the boat sails smooth, if you catch my drift", Brad debriefed Chris as they made their way back upstairs to call it a night after a long hard day.

<u>~June 5th~</u>

(6:37am)

Chris thoroughly cleaned out the baby jars as Brad wrapped up the top of their work table with plastic reynolds wrap.

"Make sure you completely clean and dry off the eye droppers", Brad instructed while taking the bread pan out of the refrigerator.

Brad took the fermented bread out of the bread pan and smashed it out evenly over the entire table.

"Hey, that kind of looks like looking into space", Chris exclaimed as he walked up and stood beside his partner in crime.

"Pull up a bar stool and get comfortable buddy, cause we're gonna be here for a while", Brad told his assistant, refering to the long task they had ahead of them for the day.

"Tweezers please", Brad requested, holding out his hand as if he was performing surgery.

"So all we gotta do now Chris is pick out all of the purple and white crystals that you see in the bread and place them on the black construction paper", Brad directed as the two of them combed through the smashed out bread before them.

(12:21 am)

"You said that it would take all day, but I didn't think that you literally meant all day", Chris complained as he started back picking out the tiny little crystals one by one of what seemed to be a neverending assignment after their brief lunch break.

Once the boys finished picking out all of the crystals, Chris separated the crystals into two separate color groups and then put the purple and white crystals into two separate baby food jars.

As Chris carefully divided the crystals, Brad began to measure out the purified water so it could matched with the crystals, volume for volume, and then slowly began to pour the water into the jar that contained the purple crystals.

"It looks like mud", Chris remarked as he watched Brad mix the two together.

Once Brad completed mixing the water and the crystals together, they both grabbed an eye dropper each, along with ten preforated sheets of paper, and began cautiously dropping an eye drop of the muddy looking water onto each square of the preforated galaxy paper.

(9:48pm)

"This right here my man is easily ten grand in the bank", Brad told Chris as they stood back and looked at the galaxy paper as it hung drying.

"We don't have to watch it dry do we?", Chris asked, more than ready to go upstairs, take a shower, and jump right into the bed and sleep forever.

" Not unless you want to sit down here in this dungen for another four to five hours just looking at the designs on the paper", Brad replied as they cleaned up their work area and restored unused supplies.

"So what do we do with the jar with the white crystals in it?", Chris inquired.

"Give it to your girlfriend to help them kill some of them big rats they got running around their house", Brad jokingly replied as the boys made their way back up the stairs and into the house for the night.

-June 6th-

(11:16am)

Brad paced back and forth wondering how could he test the acid without actually testing it himself.

His first thought was to test it on the dog, but that thought quickly diminished when he realized that the dog wouldn't be able to tell him what effects the acid had on him.

His second thought was to trick Chris into testing it unknowingly by making some sandwiches and putting a sticker into the sandwich he would have planted him and just wait to see what would happen.

His third thought was to just wait and find a test dummy from school or something.

With anticipation eating him alive, Brad quickly went back to his second thought and began making some sandwiches for him and his roommate. Brad then watched TV and patiently waited for Chris to come down stairs so the test could begin.

As planned, Chris came down stairs and flopped down into the love seat adjacent from where Brad was sitting watching TV while nibbling on his sandwich.

"I hope this one is for me Dr. Jekyll?", Chris inquired of the other sandwich sitting on the coffee table.

"Sure, if you want it, not that you won't gonna eat it anyway", Brad replied in his normal sarcastic way, laying his head back on the couch continuing to seemingly watch TV while patiently awaiting for Chris to go on the trip of his life.

"When Death Becomes Life"

<u>The Drought...</u>

(Black Creek, North Carolina, 12:20am)

The young boy tossed and turned in his sleep, desperately fighting with the nightmares in which seemed to have had a suffocating grasp upon him.

Sweat poured from his pores as he struggled to pronounce the words which his lips refused to let escape into verbal freedom.

Silent sighs overshadowed the mumbling of his creolized gibberish, thus stifling his stagnated speech, which seemingly could only be understood by the author of language himself.

Vivid visions played out in slow motion as the mental mirages of his young mind drifted from the realistic realms of misunderstanding to manifestation.

Verbatim, he unconsciously quoted within his sleep a scripture in which he had heard his grandfather recite so many times before, "Then was the secret revealed unto Daniel in a night vision. Then Daniel blessed the God of Heaven".

(Gonaives, Haiti, 11:21pm)

Riots raged as the war for food and survival spilled out into the blood drenched flooded streets of Gonaives, Haiti.

Soldiers unavailingly attempted to maintain some sense of chaotic order to a civilized people of restless revolution.

"Hurry, hurry, this way!", a tall lanky man demanded of the little boy whom just stood in shock as if his young eyes were seeing what his mind couldn't comprehend.

"Come now little one before you get yourself trampled by the stamped", the man pleaded, taking hold of the young boys hand and pulling him into the back door of what was once an old farmers market, but which now just served as a place of temporary shelter and refuge.

Standing in a darkened room, the young boy tried to bring some sense of reasonable clarity to what only appeared to him as a vague dream, but all his perusing eyes could find was his emotional mirages of fear and confusion.

"Is this the newest member of the foundation?", a deep voice within the unseen distance questioned.

"Are you a scientist also young man?", another voice jokingly asked from the opposite side of the dim room.

"No sir, but I want to be, I want to be a weather man so I can make it rain", the young boy replied with such assurance, confirming that he was indeed somehow in the right place, but at a bad time.

"Make it rain, now why in the world would a youngling have a mind set to want to make it rain?" the voice directly over the boy's shoulder inquired, as all the voices in the room began to laugh in unison at the young boy's dreams and aspirations.

"Cause sir, my grandpa said he can't grow no more food cause the dirt is too dry, so we need it to rain. He's been praying and praying for rain, but no rain has come yet, so I thought that maybe I can help him", the young boy explained, intriguing the elders curiosity to compose a quest of questions in which the circle of scholars had often asked themselves.

"What is your name son?" Dr. LaTourette asked of the young boy whom he had pulled from out of the streets of snafu only moments ago.

"Daniel Fortee' sir, but my grandpa just call me Junior, cause that was my daddie's name too", the boy answered.

"So Daniel, what makes you think that you can help your grandpa, why do you believe that you can make it rain?" Dr. LaTourette continued to inquire of the young boy whom was now known to him as Daniel Fortee' Jr.

"Cause I dreamed I did, and my grandpa always use to say that the secret was revealed to me in a night vision, and then I blessed the God of heaven and earth", Daniel proclaimed with such sincerity, silencing the skepticism of all whom doubted his silencing the skepticism of all whom doubted his destiny.

"Ok then, all in favor to induct Mr. Fortee' Jr. as the newest member of the foundation, pleas say aye and raise your hand", Dr. LaTourette requested of all the members whom was gathered within the small room.

"Aye!", all seven of the men's voices sounded in harmony, welcoming their newest and youngest comrade into the foundation of Haitian scientists.

(Friday, 12:37am)

Reverend Moses Fortee' sat up in his bed in attempt to decipher the unusual sounds coming from his grandson's bedroom, while urging his wife to awake in order to confirm that his ears were not deceiving him.

"Adell, Adell, wake up Adell and listen to that boy in there talking like he got demons in him", Reverend Moses proclaimed to his wife of their grandson whom was in the neighboring room talking in his sleep, speaking some sort of demonic sounding unidentified foreign language.

"Go to sleep Moses, ain't nothing wrong with that boy, he's probably just having a nightmare or something. As a matter of fact, sometimes you do the same thang when you sleep", Adell demanded of her husband to let their grandson be.

"I'm telling you Adell, that boy ain't been the same since his mamma and daddy got killed, It's something wrong with him, listen to him, that ain't no regular talk for nobody, especially for somebody his age", Moses continued to argue his point upon deaf ears.

"Go to sleep Moe", Adell demanded for the last time before rolling over and closing her eyes for the remainder of the night.

(Thursday, 11:40pm)

The council gathered, including their newest member and intern, Mr. Daniel Fortee' Jr.

Secretary of information, Dr. Etienne, read the minutes of their last meeting, including their projected plans for the next few weeks to come.

"Our ultimate goal is to discover a method in which we have the ability to regulate rainfall", head scientist and founder of The Foundation of Haitian Scientists, Dr. LaTourette stated, looking around the table at his colleagues, opening the floor for any thoughts or concerns pertaining to their matter at hand.

Cutting through a brief moment of silence, the newbie sharply raised his hand with an apparent look of confusion upon his face.

"Yes Mr. Fortee' Jr., please share your thoughts", Dr. LaTourette responded to Daniel through a mist of admirable giggles.

"But if you got a flood, then why would you want to make it rain?", Daniel asked in a childish way, but with the notion of an old man.

"I guess the boy is much more intuitive than what we imagined", secretary of defense, Dr. Aristide laughed with amusement.

"Well Mr. Fortee', your concerns are definitely an understandable one, but please realize, we don't so much desire to make it rain at this moment, but we do desire to discover a method by which we can regulate the rain, meaning, so we can make it rain when we want it to rain for farmers such as your grandfather", Dr. LaTourette explained to the young boy in terms that he could understand, as well as the rest of the council which sat assembled. "But ironically Dr. LaTourette, the boy makes a good point", Director of Operations, Dr. Perera, interjected, "Instead of regulating the rainfall, shouldn't our main focus be more geared towards soil absorption and the prevention of erosion, which is indeed the primary factor of flooding, just as well as a drought", Dr. Perera continued, stating what seemed to be the obvious.

"Point understood, Dr. Perera, and we must surely take your concerns into account, for it would truly kill two birds with one stone, metaphorically speaking. But with the ability to regulate rainfall, there would be no need to have a concern for soil absorption", Dr. LaTourette agreeingly disagreed, elaborating on his ideology and reasoning, before being interrupted by Dr. Beltrande.

"But with all due respect, Dr. LaTourette, to regulate rainfall would mean having the ability to start and stop the rainfall at our will. So my question is, even if we could make it rain, which does seem scientifically possible, how do we manage to stop it from raining?", Dr. Beltrande inquired, causing some of his colleges to sit back in their seats and ponder the obstacles in which he had just placed on the table of the council.

"Well with all due respect to you as well, Dr. Beltrande, that's what you are here for, and that's why you're the Minister of Research and Information, so when you find your first clue, please keep us informed", Dr. LaTourette sarcastically replied to his long time friend and college before calling the meeting to a close.

"So if there aren't any more questions or concerns to be presented at this point and time, let us bring this meeting to a close, with the expectations of us all meeting here Friday morning to prepare for our expedition into the dwindling rainforests of Port-au-Prince. Please be prompt gentlemen, so until then, God bless and have a safe week", Dr. LaTourette pleaded his closing remarks as he grabbed his belongings preparing to leave.

"Can I go?", the young boy eagerly asked of his mentor and guardian, "Please!"

"Sure son, but for now, let us go so you will be well rested for school tomorrow", Dr. LaTourette assured Daniel, patting him on his back as they walked out through the door and into the night.

(Sally B. Howard Middle School)

"Is there something more interesting outside than what I'm teaching in here Daniel?" Mrs. Sutton questioned, noticing that Daniel's attention was being abducted by something outside of her classroom window.

"Yes ma'am, I mean, no ma'am, I mean, not really", Daniel stutterantly replied with a mixture of confusion and shock.

"Well which is it Mr. Fortee'?, I only asked you one question, cause it's obvious that you're not paying any attention to me, so please feel free to share with me and the rest of the class what's so intriguing that you can't seem to focus in here", Mrs. Sutton interrogated Daniel with a sass of sarcasm, giving him the undivided attention of the entire class, that of which she didn't seem to receive from him.

"I'm sorry Mrs. Sutton, I was just looking at the rain on the window and wondering how could it be raining on the window if it's not raining outside", the young boy sincerely replied with an question, almost compelling Mrs. Sutton to apologize to him as well.

"Well being that this is a science class, I guess that's a legitimate question. And being that it does pertain to science and education, let's see if we can find you that answer", Mrs. Sutton mildly responded, attempting to bring ease to what felt as an uncomfortable situation for both him and her.

"Thanks Mrs. Sutton", Daniel exclaimed, sitting straight up in his seat with a great big smile on his face.

As Mrs. Sutton made her way to the chalk board preparing to breakdown the elements of condensation, Daniel grabbed his pen and paper, ready to record every word that Mrs. Sutton was going to write and say.

"I see you're very eager and interested about this Daniel", Mrs. Sutton stated the obvious, "So may I ask why is it that you're so interested in what you call rain on a window".

"So I can make it rain so my grandpa can keep growing food, cause he said, with no rain, there's no food", he told her, "And you know what Mrs. Sutton?, I'm even going to a rainforest this weekend with some more scientists to find out how to regulate rainfall", Daniel continued to explain with all the honesty a young boy his age could have, through the giggles and laughs of everyone in the classroom, including Mrs. Sutton.

"Well I don't know about all of that Daniel, but what I can tell you and the rest of the class is that, condensation, or rain as you call it, is when water changes from a vapor into a liquid", Mrs. Sutton began to explain before being interrupted.

"Is that the same kind of water vapor that the trees breathe Mrs. Sutton?" Daniel interjected his curiosity.

"I'm not certain about that one Daniel, but it is when warm air rises and cools to the point it is no-longer hot enough to stay a vapor, so therefore, the invisible water vapor changes and becomes a visible water droplet." Mrs. Sutton continued to inform the class until the sounding of the bell.

"Alright class, I will see you all Monday" Mrs. Sutton yelled upon deaf ears as the kids hurried out of the classroom to start their long awaited weekend.

"Daniel, can I see you for one second please sir?" Mrs. Sutton requested, "Now I admire your youthful imagination, but please understand that it's a fine line between fiction and fibbing, okay?" she told him, feeling compassionate about his apparent depressive state due to the loss of his parents a few months ago.

"No ma'am Mrs. Sutton, I'm not storying, I promise I'm not, I am going to a rainforest this weekend" Daniel pleaded his case to the woman whom was much more than a teacher to him.

"Okay Daniel, well go before you miss your bus, and I'll see you at church on Sunday" she told him, waving him goodbye as he ran out the door as if he was chasing down his bus. "Lord I hope that boy will be alright", Ms. Sutton mumbled to herself, knowing that he would need to see the counselor soon.

(Back at the house)

Moses sat silently on his front porch with his childhood friend, Roy Rogers, as they both gazed over their field of dreams, just praying for some rain to counter the hot summers days.

The crops barely stood, sun burned and dehydrated from the lack of rain, seeming as if a miracle would be the only chance the harvest had to be saved from the destruction of the drought.

"Well Roy, I've done all I know to do, and been praying the best I know how both day and night. I guess it's like it was written, for there surely hasn't been any dew nor rain in these last few months, so it's all in the Lords hands now, just as it has always been", Moses told his lifelong friend, still looking over the fields with tears in his eyes while just shaking his head in bewilderment.

"Don't know any Indians do you Moe? I know you of all people know that God blessed Elijah to make it rain, you know, when Elijah danced for the rain to come on top of that mountain, and that hand came up out of the ocean and it rained for forty days and nights, remember that don't you?" Roy asked within a giggle, attempting to break some of the seriousness of what was becoming a somber moment.

"Naw, I don't remember that Roy, But I do get your point, but just to let you know cause you're my friend, you just put about five different events from four different chapters of the Bible all together in one", Moses told Roy as they both began to laugh and dance, imitating the ancient rain dance of the Native Americans.

During a brief intermission to catch their breath from reenacting the Indians cry for rain, Daniel excitingly ran up on the porch with his book bag dragging behind him.

"Boy what you so excited about? And pick that bag up on your shoulders like you suppose too", Moses stopped his grandson dead in his tracks as soon as he hit the top step of the porch.

"Gotta go and pack for my trip to the rainforest grandpa, I"mma learn how to make it rain, I'mma save your plants grandpa, they gonna teach me how", Daniel told his Grandpa in a series of fragmented sentences while gasping to catch his breath in between each, due to the hundred yard dash he had just ran from the bus at the end of their path.

"Sounds like your grandboy is gonna be the answer to your prayers Moe, just wish he woulda told us thabefore we did all of that rain dancing and carrying on", Roy expressed to Moses in a mix of sporadic chuckles, pointing at the young boy wonder whom sincerely believed that he was destined to save the day.

"Now, Roy, you know how these childrens are with their wild imaginations", Moses mildly said to his friend without saying what he really wanted to say in front of his grandson.

"Go in the house, boy, and take off them school clothes", Moses continued, turning his attention away from Roy's sarcastic comment, to his grandson whom was standing before him with a disappointed smile upon his face.

"I'm telling you, Roy, something strange is going on with that boy, I've been telling that stubborn wife of mine that that boy ain't been the same since his ma' and pa' got killed in that car accident. And of course, she won't listen, and here you are making a mockery out of it all, I'm telling y'all, that boy need some professional help", Moses pleaded his case to Roy with such heart felt sincerity that all Roy could do was shake his head in agreement and apologize to his dear old friend. Hearing all of the ramping and raging of her husband out on the front porch, Adell stuck her head out the screen door to see what was all the fuse about.

The more she heard, the more she doubted if she should tell her husband about the phone call she had just received from Mrs. Sutton concerning Daniels tall tale about going on an excursion to a rainforest, and making it rain.

At third thought, Adell opted not to tell her

husband for the fear of him overreacting as he usually does. So without saying a single word to Moses, she just glanced at Roy with that familiar, "Here we go again", look on her face.

(Later that same Night)

Daniel threw his book bag full of clothes and knick-knacks up against the headboard, climbed up into his bed, and patiently awaited for his expedition another realm of reality.

"Are you ready Mr. Fortee' Jr.?" Dr. LaTourette rhetorically questioned the young boy whom looked so eager to begin the journey in which he had so anxiously awaited for.

"Yes sir", Daniel simply replied with a bright smile on his face, snapping in the buckle of his book bag around his waist.

"And what about the rest of you gentlemen?" Dr. LaTourette inquired of the others, only to be answered in return by a few gesturing head nods and some silent yesses.

(This is where you become The Co-Author
and decide how the story ends.)

"When Dreams Become Reality"

Booking Information

~ Sean Ingram ~

Author ~ Spoken Word Artist ~ Song Writer ~ Inspirational Speaker

www.SeanIngram.info

email@SeanIngram.info

myspace.com/TheSeanIngramSociety

* Please visit our online book club, as well as The Critics Corner, where you can read or post your very own book reviews or comments to Sean Ingram.

Also Available by Sean Ingram

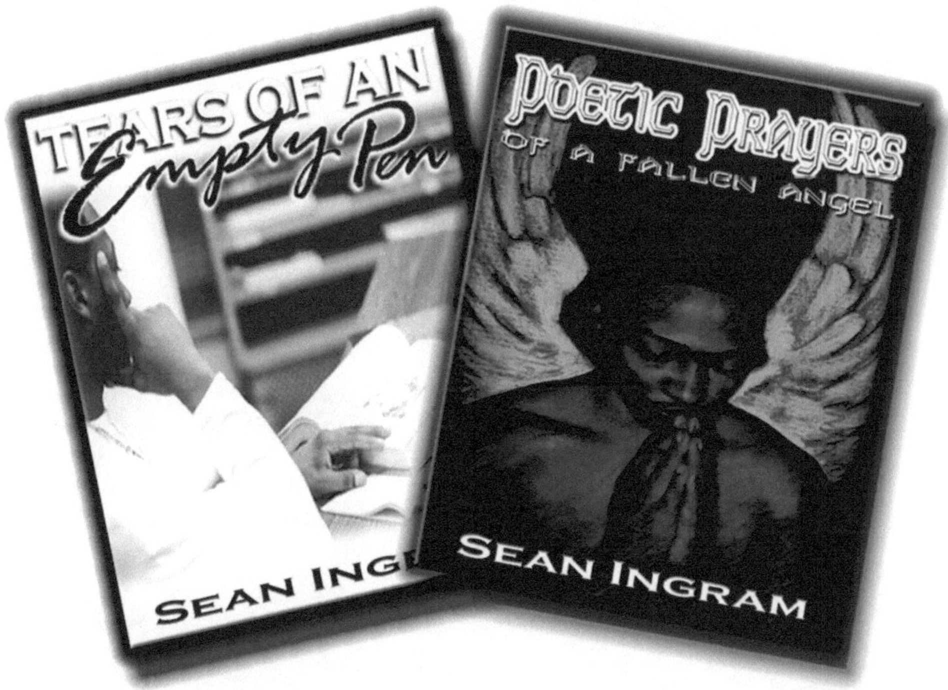

In Book Stores Now!

www.SeanIngram.info

www.ingramcontent.com/pod-product-compliance
Lightning Source LLC
Chambersburg PA
CBHW022204050726
47590CB00002B/627